PIMLICO

489

IN THE LAND OF WHITE DEATH

Valerian Albanov was born in 1881 in Voronezh, Russia, and graduated in 1904 from the Naval College of St. Petersburg. Despite his harrowing voyage aboard the *Saint Anna*, he continued going to sea until his death in 1919.

Jon Krakauer is the bestselling author of *Into the Wild* and *Into Thin Air*, and was a finalist for the Pulitzer Prize in 1998.

David Roberts is the author of over a dozen books on mountaineering, exploration, and archaeology, including, most recently, *True Summit*. His work regularly appears in *National Geographic Adventure*, *Smithsonian*, and *Outside*, among other publications.

Valerian Ivanovich Albanov

IN THE LAND OF WHITE DEATH

An Epic Story of Survival
in the Siberian Arctic

VALERIAN ALBANOV

Preface by Jon Krakauer

Introduction by David Roberts

Alison Anderson, Translator

With additional material from William Barr's translation
from the Russian

PIMLICO

Published by Pimlico 2001

2 4 6 8 10 9 7 5 3

Grateful acknowledgement is made to William Barr for permission to incorporate some
material from his largely unpublished English translation of *In the Land of White Death* by
Valerian Albanov.
Copyright © 2000 by William Barr. Used by permission.

First published in Great Britain by Pimlico 2001

Pimlico
Random House, 20 Vauxhall Bridge Road,
London SW1V 2SA

Random House Australia (Pty) Limited
20 Alfred Street, Milsons Point, Sydney,
New South Wales 2061, Australia

Random House New Zealand Limited
18 Poland Road, Glenfield,
Auckland 10, New Zealand

Random House (Pty) Limited
Endulini, 5A Jubilee Road, Parktown 2193, South Africa

The Random House Group Limited Reg. No. 954009
www.randomhouse.co.uk

A CIP catalogue record for this book
is available from the British Library

ISBN 0-7126-6815-2

Papers used by Random House UK Limited are natural,
recyclable products made from wood grown in sustainable forests.
The manufacturing processes conform to the environmental
regulations of the country of origin.

Printed and bound in Great Britain by
Biddles Ltd, Guildford

PREFACE

Jon Krakauer

When Robert Falcon Scott perished on an Antarctic glacier in 1912, just eleven miles from salvation, he was ven-
erated as one of the foremost fallen heroes in the history
of the British Empire. There is scarcely a schoolboy in all
of Britannia who can't recite the story of Scott's ill-
starred quest by heart.

Three years after Scott so famously came to grief, an expedition to Antarctica under the leadership of Ernest
Shackleton seemed headed for a similarly grim end. Shackleton's ship, the *Endurance*, was crushed by ice and sank,
leaving twenty-eight men stranded on the frozen Weddell
Sea. Shackleton, however, managed to deliver his entire
team to safety, by means of an audacious eight-hundred-
mile voyage across the gale-ravaged South Atlantic Ocean
in a puny open lifeboat. This near-miraculous journey was
recently made familiar to millions of readers by such de-
servedly popular books as *Endurance*, by Alfred Lansing,
and *The Endurance*, by Caroline Alexander. Shackleton's

name became synonymous with courage, tenacity, and brilliant leadership under pressure.

All of which begs the question: If Scott and Shackleton have attained such posthumous stature and renown, why is Valerian Ivanovich Albanov all but unknown to the world?

Albanov was a Russian navigator. In 1912, six months after the death of Scott, he set sail from Alexandrovsk (present-day Murmansk) as second in command on the good ship *Saint Anna,* bound for Vladivostok, 7,000 miles away, across treacherous Arctic waters. Some two years before Shackleton's *Endurance* was beset by pack ice off Antarctica, Albanov's *Saint Anna* was likewise trapped at the opposite end of the globe, in the frozen Kara Sea. Eighteen months later, with supplies running perilously low and his vessel more firmly locked in the ice than ever, Albanov abandoned ship and led thirteen men southward in a desperate fight for survival.

The trials Albanov endured as he struggled his way back to civilization were every bit as harrowing as those faced by Shackleton. And Albanov's story is perhaps even more riveting to read, because it is told in Albanov's own voice, as entries in a daily journal. (In contrast, the recent bestselling accounts of Shackleton's ordeal—though wonderful—were written many decades after the fact, by authors who weren't present during the events they describe.) Albanov, moreover, turned out to be both a gifted writer and an uncommonly honest diarist. He wrote a spare, astounding, utterly compelling book that—thanks to bad luck and the vagaries of history—vanished into the recesses of twentieth-century letters.

But it remains in the shadows no longer. Here, published in English for the first time, is *In the Land of White Death*. More than eighty years after Albanov wrote this tour de force, there is reason to hope that he might finally receive the recognition he deserves.

———

JON KRAKAUER is the bestselling author of *Into the Wild* and *Into Thin Air*, and was a finalist for the Pulitzer Prize in 1998.

The Saint Anna *upon its departure from St. Petersburg*

INTRODUCTION

David Roberts

How is it possible that the story of the 1912–14 voyage of the *Saint Anna,* one of the most tragic and heroic episodes in Arctic annals, remains virtually unknown outside of Russia? Even more regrettable, how can it be that the narrative of that expedition, written by one of its two survivors, Valerian Ivanovich Albanov, lurks in a limbo of historical obscurity? For Albanov's account is one of the rare masterpieces of polar literature, deserving of comparison with the classic texts of Fridtjof Nansen, Robert Falcon Scott, Apsley Cherry-Garrard, and Sir Ernest Shackleton. Yet with this edition, Albanov appears in English for the first time.

Although I have been a devotee of Arctic and Antarctic exploration for three decades, until 1997 I had never heard a word about the ill-starred journey of the *Saint Anna,* commanded by Georgiy Brusilov, nor of Albanov's daring flight from the doomed ship across the ice in quest of salvation. In Jeannette Mirsky's definitive history of northern exploration, *To the Arctic!,* Brusilov's expedition merits a mere sentence and a half, and that only to record the fruitless search for the lost party by a more famous explorer.

Three years ago, a French publisher, Michel Guérin, recommended to me an obscure book, published in French in 1928, called *Au pays de la mort blanche.* He in turn had been tipped off by Christian de Marliave, a seasoned explorer and connoisseur of polar literature. At Harvard's Widener Library, I found a copy of this French edition of Albanov, whose account in Russian was originally published in 1917. During the sixty-eight years the book had stood in the Widener stacks, it had never been checked out!

I read Albanov with a sense of awe laced with a growing excitement, for it is a stunning revelation to discover a great work in a field of writing in which one thinks one knows all the canonic books. It is thus a pleasure to introduce this neglected narrative to a new audience, and to muse on what circumstances allowed Albanov to write so vividly about the Arctic nightmare he barely survived.

There are reasons why the *Saint Anna* story has slipped through the cracks. A moderately experienced navigator in northern waters, Brusilov was uninterested in exploration for its own sake. The rationale for his expedition was to find new hunting grounds for walrus, seal, polar bear, and whale. The enterprise seems to have been jinxed from the start. A trusted friend whom Brusilov wished to make second in command, and who was bringing with him much-needed expedition funds, a doctor, and a small library of Arctic books, failed to reach the port of Alexandrovsk in time to embark. Brusilov was delayed and impoverished by an absurd Russian law that levied a crushing tax on any ship purchased in another country (in the *Saint Anna*'s case, Great Britain). As he filled his ship with twenty-three crewmates, he managed to recruit only five genuine sailors. The rest of the team members were at best professional hunters, at worst opportunists hoping to strike it rich in the fur trade.

Brusilov was demoralized by his setbacks. In his last letter, mailed to his mother from Alexandrovsk, he wrote, "Here we have had nothing but disagreements.... The ambiance was dismal: one man who fell ill, others who refused to embark...."

Nevertheless, Brusilov launched his voyage in a state of blasé overconfidence that in retrospect seems unfathomable. In proposing to emerge at Vladivostok, the captain intended to make only the second successful traverse of the Northeast Passage. Like its cousin, the more famous Northwest Passage ranging the Arctic Ocean north of Canada and Alaska, the Northeast Passage had been hypothesized since the Renaissance as a shortcut from Europe to China. The long ocean voyage to the north of Scandinavia and Siberia was first attempted by a British expedition in 1553. The perilous traverse was not completed, however, until 1879, by the great Swedish explorer Baron Nils Adolf Erik Nordenskiöld. During the thirty-three years that yawned between Nordenskiöld and Brusilov, the feat had not been repeated.

For his riffraff crew of twenty-three, Brusilov loaded on board enough provisions to feed thirty men for eighteen months, but he inexplicably failed to include adequate supplies of the antiscorbutics of the day, such as citrus fruits. Within four months, the crew of the *Saint Anna* had succumbed to a veritable plague of scurvy. Nor did Brusilov embark with nearly enough fuel to run the ship's engines and heat its cabins for two years. With all his delays, he set out on August 28, 1912, a date so late in the summer that it guaranteed the ship would be trapped in the ice.

At the last minute, Brusilov took on board a young woman named Yerminiya Zhdanko, even though the presence of females on Arctic expeditions was virtually unprecedented. With some training as a nurse, Zhdanko, Brusilov thought, might serve in place of the absent doctor. The fatal casualness with which the whole team approached the journey emerges poignantly in a letter the woman wrote her father shortly before embarking:

> The brother of Ksénia [i.e., Brusilov] has bought a boat, a schooner, it seems. He's organizing an expedition to Arkhangel'sk and is inviting passengers (it was even announced in the papers) in the event that there are enough cabins. This will take two or three weeks and I'll come home from Arkhangel'sk by train. The goal of the expedition, it seems, is to hunt walruses, bears, etc.... and then they'll try to traverse to Vladivostok, but you can be sure, none of that concerns me.

Seduced by the delight of the first leg of the journey, Zhdanko stayed aboard and sailed on to her icebound death sentence.

Above all, Brusilov underestimated the treachery of the Kara Sea, the frigid ocean north of the delta of the river Ob. As Jeannette Mirsky writes, "Since sailors first looked on the Kara Sea, it was never mentioned without an adjective denoting dread or terror; it is the 'ice-cellar.' " Yet Brusilov cavalierly coasted into this trap on September 4. By October 15, the *Saint Anna* was locked in sea ice.

At this point, the party was still close to land, for the Yamal Peninsula protruded just east of the ship. On a shore excursion, crewmen had found the fresh tracks of sleds pulled by the reindeer of the Samoyeds, nomadic natives of Siberia. Had the team abandoned the ship and fled south into the interior, every last member's life would likely have been spared. But Brusilov had not set out along the Northeast Passage to quit at the first setback. It was almost routine for a ship in Arctic waters to be frozen in for the winter, only to be disgorged into open sea in the next summer's thaw; Nordenskiöld himself had endured just such an immobilization.

So the *Saint Anna* drifted in lazy zigzags north. The team wintered over in the ice, but when the summer of 1913 came and went without freeing the ship, the disheartened crew faced the inevitability of a second winter in their Arctic prison. After a year and a half, the ship had drifted north some 2,400 miles from where it had frozen in. It had been sixteen months since the crew had last sighted land. At a latitude of 82°58′, in fact, the *Saint Anna* lay north of any terra firma in the Eastern Hemisphere.

By January 1914, there was mutiny in the air. Although there was plenty of food still on board, the coal and wood had been exhausted. The only source of heat and light was a putrid mixture of bear and seal fat with machine oil that burned with a smoky sputter. Virtually every crewmember had been incapacitated for long stretches with scurvy. To more than half the team, the prospect of waiting for a second summer's deliverance seemed tantamount to resigning themselves to the "white death" of Albanov's title.

Second in command as chief navigation officer, Valerian Albanov was, at thirty-two, three years older than his captain, with more experience in Arctic waters. By early 1914, Brusilov and his navigator had been at serious odds for months. As Albanov writes, every time the two men made contact, "the air was electric." Albanov had become convinced that the only chance for survival was to leave the ship and head, however desperately, by ski and sledge and kayak for Franz Josef Land, which the team knew lay somewhere to the south.

The only map of these little-known precincts the team possessed was a page from Fridtjof Nansen's *Farthest North*, nearly twenty years out of date, with most of the Franz Josef islands indicated by hypothetical dotted lines. Had Brusilov done his homework, or had the Arctic library his comrade intended to bring aboard the ship actually arrived, the captain would have known that in 1900, after reaching a new farthest north, the great Italian explorer the Duke of the Abruzzi had left an ample depot of supplies on Prince Rudolf Island, the most northerly (and for the team, the nearest) land in all of the Franz Josef archipelago. That knowledge alone might have saved the team's lives.

On January 9, 1914, Albanov requested permission from the commander he had come to hate to build a kayak. It was his intention to flee the ship on his own, but within the month, many of his teammates were inspired to follow his example. Brusilov consented, mindful of how much longer the dwindling food supply would last with half his crewmembers gone.

It would have been one thing had a foresighted captain stowed kayaks and sledges aboard for just such an emergency. Instead, Albanov and his cronies had to improvise kayaks and sledges out of the materials at hand. It is a testimonial to these sailors' remarkable craftsmanship that a pair of kayaks and a pair of sledges ultimately held up till very near the end of the ordeal.

On April 10, 1914, Albanov and thirteen companions set off across the sea ice, leaving the *Saint Anna* behind. Three of the party soon thought better of their flight and returned to the ship. With him, Albanov carried a copy of Brusilov's log, which recorded in brief, unimaginative entries the appalling year and a half of helpless drift.

The reader may well wonder why Brusilov and so many of his teammates were content to linger on board the ice-locked ship. One piece of Arctic history the captain did know was the strange fate of the *Jeannette*, an American ship that had been trapped by ice in 1879 north of eastern Siberia. A year and a half later, the polar pack dealt its death blow to the *Jeannette*, crushing and sinking her. Forced to head for land six hundred miles away, thirteen of the party's thirty-three men, including the expedition leader, perished either on the ice or in improvised refuges on forlorn shores.

Three years after this disaster, recognizable pieces of the *Jeannette* washed up on the shores of Greenland. Thus explorers learned of the unexpected large-scale currents that governed the drift of polar ice. In 1893, in what was arguably the boldest Arctic expedition ever launched, the visionary Norwegian Fridtjof Nansen took advantage of this discovery to prosecute a wildly ambitious attempt on the North Pole.

Nansen had a ship designed with a shallow, rounded keel, so that instead of being gripped and crushed by the ice, it would be thrust upward by the pressure of the floes. Then he sailed off north of Siberia with the deliberate aim of getting the *Fram* frozen into the pack. The design worked: The ship's keel slid safely above the frozen sea. After the *Fram* had drifted erratically northwest for a year and a half, Nansen and a single companion set off with dogs to ski to the Pole. They had no hope of regaining the ship.

After twenty-six days, the two men reached a new farthest north of 86°13.6′, but fickle southerly currents defeated them. Undaunted, Nansen and his partner made their way south to Franz Josef Land, wintered over a third time, and made their way to an outpost at Cape Flora, where an English explorer had built huts. They were picked up by a passing ship in August 1896. Meanwhile, the *Fram,* just as planned, had drifted with the ice all the way across the Arctic and was released unharmed into the Atlantic.

On board the *Saint Anna,* Nansen's magisterial account of that expedition, *Farthest North,* had become a kind of bible. Albanov had read certain passages so many times he had virtually memorized them. And Brusilov loitered on deck toward his second icebound summer in the serene faith that the drifting pack would liberate the *Saint Anna* just as it had the *Fram*.

———

Most of the finest polar narratives are leisurely, richly detailed, grandly symphonic works (Apsley Cherry-Garrard's *The Worst Journey in the World,* the definitive account of Scott's tragic 1910–13 Antarctic expedition, runs to 643 pages in the Penguin edition). *In the Land of White Death,* however, is as lean and taut as a good thriller. One of the felicities of Albanov's book is his decision to begin his account with his departure from the *Saint Anna* on April 10, 1914. The whole of the dolorous but uneventful drift of the ship frozen into the ice the author wisely ignores.

Thus the book narrows its focus to the ninety-day ordeal during which, commanded by Albanov, ten men struggled through unimaginable hardships and dangers to traverse 235 miles of frozen sea, open leads, glaciers, and island shores to gain the same Cape Flora that had proved Nansen's deliverance. Among other accomplishments, Albanov's escape was a brilliant feat of navigation, for with only a faulty chronometer, he had no way of divining an accurate longitude. During one agonizing moment midway in the journey, the pilot had to guess whether the whole of Franz Josef Land lay east or west of him. He guessed east, and he was right.

Albanov was a born leader. Without him, the other men would have died early on. Growing sick of the tedious alternation of kayaking open leads with the sledges as baggage and man-hauling the sledges with kayaks stowed, five of the men urged abandoning both kayaks and sledges and skiing hell-bent for land. Albanov not only recognized that course as suicidal folly, but managed to convince his followers of the fact.

There is no denying Albanov's compassion: The sleepless vigils as he awaits absent colleagues, the retracing of his hard-won path to hunt for stragglers, give proof of his humanity. Yet at the same time, he must have been an autocratic and headstrong leader. In an age when interpersonal conflicts were politely veiled in public accounts, Albanov makes no secret of his disdain for Brusilov. Even more strikingly (and this is another strength of the book), Albanov rails in print against the apathy and incompetence of his teammates, despite the fact that as he writes in 1917, they are all but one dead. Thus "My companions are no better than children"; they are "foolish"; "I am sure they are capable of anything." When one crewman carelessly loses an invaluable Remington rifle, Albanov is so outraged that he strikes out at any teammate who crosses his path.

The hazards of that ninety-day journey, from being chased by walruses to falling through thin ice into the numbing sea, make up a gauntlet of continuous peril. The ups and downs of hope and despair measure out the psychological *agon* of the voyage. And the sheer mystery of the fate of missing comrades haunts the reader just as it haunts Albanov.

Yet many a dramatic Arctic ordeal has produced only a plodding expedition book. What is the secret of Albanov's all-but-unconscious genius as narrator?

The style is plain and direct, though rich in concrete detail. Yet in the breast of the plainspoken chronicler there also abides the soul of a poet. One of the finest passages in the book is the lyrical outburst Albanov delivers upon reaching land for the first time in almost two years. The cacophonous birdsong sounds "the hymn of life and the hymn of existence"; tiny yellow flowers were "greeting us again with their pure and charming splendor"; even the sight of innumerable small stones gleaming in the sun imparts an unspeakable joy. Yet there hangs over this idyll the unguessed tribulation of the future—for the land would prove far more fatal to Albanov's men than the sea.

With all the hindsight available to him as he took up his pen in 1917, Albanov cunningly resisted the temptation to foreshadow or moralize. He had kept a diary throughout his excruciating escape. In his book, he recasts the narrative as that diary, though without doubt the entries have been enhanced and polished (exhausted men do not write lyrical odes to refulgent nature). The effect of this strategy is to recapture in all its tense uncertainty the drama of never knowing whether a given day's actions lead one closer to safety or to death. At the most optimistic moments, the cruel Arctic knocks Albanov's party flat; yet in the depths of their discouragement, it unveils a corridor of hope.

Moreover, Albanov seems blessed with an inborn knack for metaphor. In the midst of his closest call, the iceberg on which he and his last partner, Alexander Konrad, have taken refuge cracks open and dumps the two men, trapped in a double sleeping bag, into the sea. Albanov likens their plight to that of "kittens thrown together in a sack to be drowned." The most ordinary turns in the party's grim trek push Albanov to an apostrophic eloquence, as when he hears a teammate exhort the moribund Shpakovsky, "Do you want to join Nilsen?"—the teammate who had died the day before. There follows an inspired *pensée* in which Albanov analyzes the small increments by which exhaustion leads to death. The passage serves as well as Albanov's implicit prayer for deliverance.

By the time his book was published, Albanov had only two years to live. Having survived, through improvisatory pluck and heroic perseverance, one of the most deadly of all Arctic ordeals, Albanov would perish in 1919—in only his thirty-eighth year. By some accounts he died of typhoid fever; others report that he was killed absurdly when a boxcar loaded with munitions blew up in a Russian train station. His fellow survivor, Alexander Konrad, lived until 1940.

Of the nine men who died trying to reach Cape Flora; of the thirteen, including Brusilov and Yerminiya Zhdanko, who stayed aboard the *Saint Anna;* of the doomed ship itself—not a trace was ever found.

———

DAVID ROBERTS is the author of over a dozen books on mountaineering, exploration, and archaeology, including, most recently, *True Summit.* His work regularly appears in *National Geographic Adventure, Smithsonian,* and *Outside,* among other publications.

CONTENTS

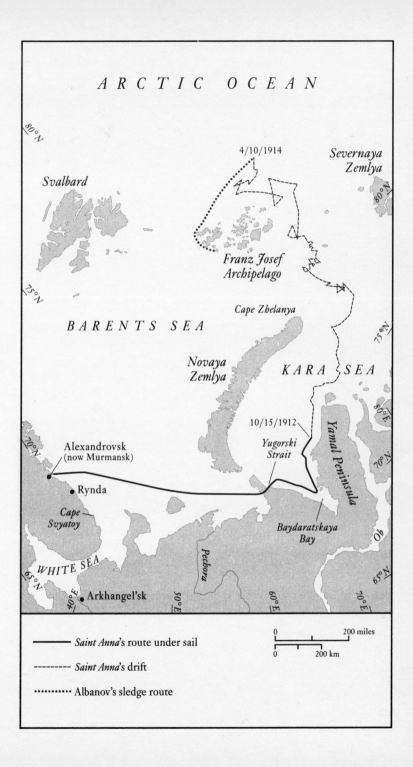

ARCTIC OCEAN

Svalbard

Severnaya
Zemlya

4/10/1914

Franz Josef
Archipelago

BARENTS SEA

Cape Zhelanya

KARA SEA

Novaya
Zemlya

Yamal Peninsula

10/15/1912

Alexandrovsk
(now Murmansk)

Yugorski
Strait

Rynda

Cape
Svyatoy

Baydaratskaya
Bay

Ob

WHITE SEA

Pechora

Arkhangel'sk

——— *Saint Anna*'s route under sail

- - - - - *Saint Anna*'s drift

·········· Albanov's sledge route

0   200 miles

0   200 km

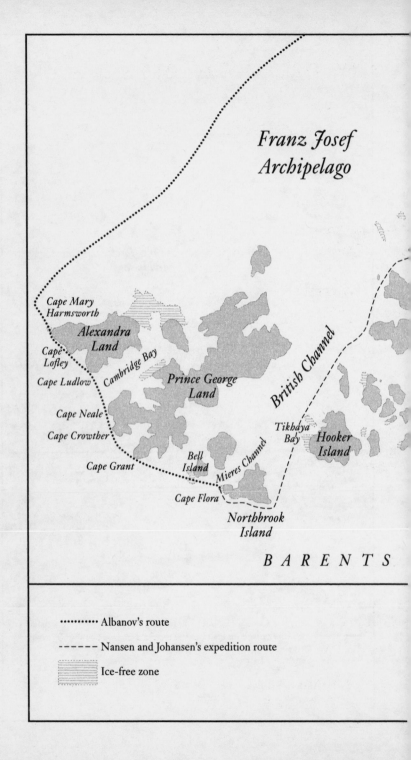

*Franz Josef
Archipelago*

Cape Mary
Harmsworth
*Alexandra
Land*
Cape
Lofley
Cape Ludlow
Cambridge Bay
*Prince George
Land*
Cape Neale
Cape Crowther
Cape Grant
Bell
Island
Mieres Channel
British Channel
Tikhaya
Bay
*Hooker
Island*
Cape Flora
*Northbrook
Island*

B A R E N T S

·········· Albanov's route

- - - - - Nansen and Johansen's expedition route

Ice-free zone

ARCTIC OCEAN

Cape Fligely

Prince Rudolf
Island

Hvidtenland

Frederick Jackson
Island

Ziegler
Island

Graham Bell
Island

Wilczek
Land

Hall
Island

McClintock
Island

SEA

0   50 miles

0   50 km

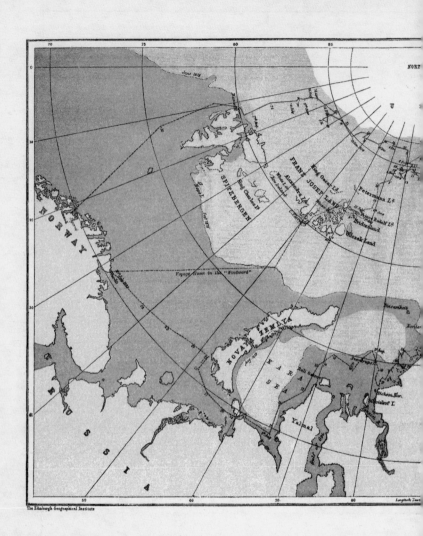

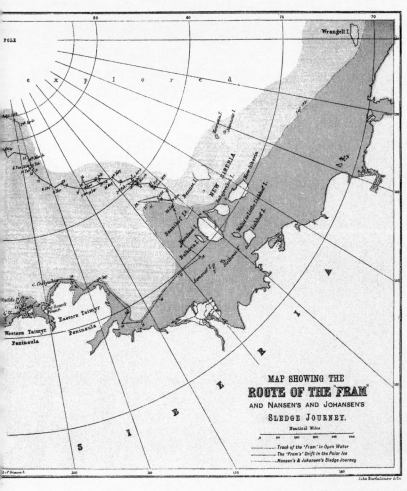

Map from Farthest North *by Fridtjof Nansen*

IN THE LAND
OF WHITE
DEATH

Why I Left the Saint Anna

How many weeks and months have gone by since the day I left the *Saint Anna* and bade farewell to Lieutenant Brusilov! Little did I know that our separation was to be forever.

The ship was completely trapped by the ice pack. She had been drifting northward for a year and a half off Franz Josef Land. In October 1912, she had become ice-bound in the Kara Sea at latitude 71°45′ north, unable to advance or retreat, at the mercy of the winds and tides.

Together with thirteen other crewmembers I left the ship to her aimless course and set off on foot toward Franz Josef Land, in search of an inhabited shore.

Although it is not overly long since I left, I find it somewhat difficult to re-create from memory a complete picture of those dismal weeks and months on board the *Saint Anna*. I have completely forgotten many incidents, but certain events remain engraved on my memory. If the diary I had kept on the ship had been saved, my narrative would of course have made use of its entire contents. But all the notes that I had entrusted to two companions on the eve of my rescue disappeared with them when they failed to reach Cape Flora on Northbrook Island in the Franz Josef archipelago. The few notes I kept on my person are intact, and cover the period from May 14 to August 10, 1914. Here follows the excerpt from Lieutenant Brusilov's logbook relating the events which caused our separation, and which I submitted upon my return to the Hydrographic Bureau of Petrograd:

September 9. I relieved the navigation officer of his duties.

January 9. Lengthened the Thomson sounding cable with a makeshift wire cable, as the 400-fathom sounding line that we had at our disposal was inadequate. Navigation Officer Albanov, whom I have relieved of his duties, asked me for permission and materials to build a kayak in which he planned to leave the ship in the springtime. Appreciating his difficult position on board, I gave my consent. Northern lights in the evening.

January 22. The ship's crew asked me to meet with them in their quarters, and when I did they also requested permission to build kayaks, following the navigation officer's example. They were afraid of spending a third winter in such perilous circumstances and with so few provisions. At first I tried to talk them out of their plan by promising that if the ship did not break free of the ice by the following summer, we too would abandon the ship and set off in our lifeboats. I reminded them of the fate of the *Jeannette*, whose crew had been forced to cover a far greater distance in their light craft, but had nevertheless managed to reach a safe port. My efforts were in vain, as none of them believed the *Saint Anna* would ever break free again, and their only desire was to see their homeland again. I announced that they could all make ready to leave if that is what they wanted. A small but increasing number of them decided to stay, more than I actually would have liked, but I did not want to force anyone to leave. Together with the nurse, those who finally remained on board were two harpooners, the engineer, the stoker, the steward, the cook, and two young sailors. I needed their services in any case to maintain and run the ship. Taking their numbers into account, our supplies should last for one year, if rationed carefully, and so in the final analysis I was quite pleased with this unexpected turn of events. My sense of responsibility had remained intact because the others were leaving voluntarily, and had freely chosen their fate....

At my request, the following paragraph explaining my reasons for leaving the *Saint Anna* was added to Brusilov's logbook: "After Lieutenant Brusilov had recovered from his long and serious illness, our relations became more and more strained to the point of becoming intolerable in our present desperate situation. As I could not foresee a solution to our conflict, I asked the lieutenant to relieve me of my duties as navigator. After some reflection Lieutenant Brusilov complied with my request, for which I am extremely grateful to him."

His own account proves beyond question that I asked to leave alone. It was only on January 22 that he informed me that certain crewmembers wished to accompany me. The only reason I wanted to leave was my personal dispute with Brusilov, whereas the others wanted to avoid spending a third winter marooned on the ice with dwindling supplies.

Now as I look back in retrospect on my quarrel with Brusilov, I can see that the pressure of our desperate situation had frayed our nerves to the breaking point. Our journey had been dogged by misfortune from the very start. Serious illness, a pervasive doubt that our fortunes would soon change, the certainty that we were at the mercy of hostile natural forces, and, finally, the growing concern about our inadequate food supply, were grounds for all manner of disagreements and flaring tempers. The minor frictions that a prolonged sharing of quarters inevitably produces drove us further and further apart, and finally created an almost insurmountable barrier between us. Neither of us made any effort to put our differences aside and let bygones be bygones. The air was electric whenever we met; an underlying hostility became more and more evident, and senseless fits of anger prevailed on every occasion. At times we quarreled so violently, for practically no reason at all, that we were left speechless and had to stay away from each other to avoid more serious outbursts. If we each had tried, after the fact, to recall exactly why we had quarreled, we would seldom have found a legitimate reason. Even after lengthy reflection I cannot remember whether, after September 1913, we ever once had a normal, civilized conversation! We were always overemotional and often broke off our discussions in a rage. Today I am certain that we would have understood one another well enough if we had both been able to stay calm. No doubt we would have agreed that in most cases there was no cause for dispute, and that a little mutual patience would have quickly improved our relationship. But that was impossible in our overwrought state. In spite of everything, however, we did not part on bad terms. The odd, unbalanced state of mind that had prevailed on the ship now seems hard to fathom....

———

The *Saint Anna* had been very well fitted out and stocked with supplies for eighteen months. There were only twenty-four crewmembers, but our supplies had been calculated for thirty. So for the time being there was no danger of shortages. During the first year, moreover, our bear hunting had been quite successful, and had added considerably to our provisions. We could therefore assume that strict management of our resources would allow the entire crew an additional year's grace, until December 1914. Bountiful hunting might have improved our situation somewhat, but in the second year we had encountered absolutely no animals to hunt, so there was no good reason to count on this.

Early in 1914, moreover, we realized that it would be impossible to free the *Saint Anna* from the ice; at best, we would drift until the autumn of 1915, more than three years after we had departed Alexandrovsk.* If we stayed on board, starvation would become a real threat by January 1915, if not sooner. In the darkness of the long polar night, a struggle against hunger carries no hope of salvation. During this season, hunting is out of the question, as all animals are in hibernation. The only certainty for those trapped in its realm is that "white death" lies in wait for them.

Although a large number of crewmen were abandoning the vessel at a time when conditions for traveling and hunting were at their most favorable, and were taking with them two months' supplies—mainly ship's biscuits—those

* Having drifted north almost to latitude 83°, the *Saint Anna* had no chance of breaking loose from the ice pack in the summer of 1914. The ship's only hope of deliverance lay in a westward drift toward the Atlantic through the winter of 1914 to 1915. See Introduction.

staying on board the *Saint Anna* would still have enough provisions to last them comfortably until the autumn of 1915. We assumed also that the ship would, in the meantime, eventually be able to reach open water somewhere between Greenland and Svalbard.

Would our departure compromise the running of the ship? Brusilov himself was of the opinion that a crew of ten was quite sufficient to man her, even on the open sea. On the other hand, our departure would add one other appreciable advantage to the rationing of supplies, namely the saving of fuel, which was perilously scarce.

There was not a single log or piece of coal left on board; all we had left for heating was bear fat and seal blubber mixed with machine oil. The samovar was kept boiling with wood from cabin walls and other nonstructural parts of the ship. During the winter of 1913 to 1914, the entire crew lived in two cabins aft, an upper one that was smaller and colder, and another on a lower deck that was quite warm because it also served as the galley. After our departure everyone would be able to live in that lower cabin, which would greatly simplify the heating problem. Their health would improve as a result, since the temperature of the other cabin rarely rose above 41° Fahrenheit during the day and easily dropped below 28° Fahrenheit at night.

Given all these circumstances, the lieutenant could only look on our departure as a blessing that would be to everyone's benefit. Nevertheless, the same uncertain future faced us all. No one could foresee who would succeed in this unequal struggle against the treacherous Arctic elements.

Preparations for the Sledge Expedition

My preparations began on January 10, 1914. There was plenty to do. Eventually we had to build seven sledges and seven kayaks, prepare our clothing, sew and repair our boots, gather together all the supplies and think of a thousand things at once. Because we lacked essential materials and proper tools, the work was extraordinarily difficult. The wood made available to us was of poor quality. We had to manufacture rivets from copper scrap; we even had to make many of the tools we required. The many wooden pieces we sawed for each kayak were first joined together with rivets, and then lashed firmly with strong twine. When fully assembled, the entire wooden skeleton was also wrapped with the twine, and then covered with canvas cut from spare sails. All this work was carried out deep in the ship's hold, where the temperature dipped as low as −36° Fahrenheit, by the faint glow of seal-oil lamps, which we called "smudge pots" because they gave off more smoke than light. Most of the work was delicate and painstaking, so it had to be done with

bare hands despite the terrible cold. Our fingers quickly became chilled to the bone and we would have to warm them
repeatedly over the lamps. In the bitter subzero temperatures, it was particularly excruciating to rivet the kayaks and
sew the sailcloth that covered them. Our homemade needles
were so cold to the touch that they burned like red-hot iron
and blistered our fingertips. We worked from early morning
until late at night, and gradually the hold was filled with
kayaks and sledges. We lightened the hard work by telling
jokes and singing songs.

Each kayak was designed to carry two men, as well as
their equipment and supplies, and each was given a name
such as "Gull," "Auk," "Snow Bunting," "Teal," and "Ful-
mar." Due to the extreme cold of the ship's hold, it was impossible to give the boats a finishing coat of paint. We solved
the problem by lowering the kayaks through a skylight in the
afterdeck into the relative warmth of the galley. For a week
it was so crowded with kayaks we could move around in the
galley only bent double, almost on all fours.

In March a small lead opened in the ice at the bow of the
ship, which widened to be twelve feet across. There we
were able to subject our small craft to sea trials, and discovered that they performed better than our clumsy tools and
materials would have allowed us to hope. The kayaks
proved to be spacious and stable. The materials were by no
means suitable, admittedly, and certainly not what we
would have chosen, but we had to use whatever was at
hand. For the longitudinal members of the frames we were
forced to use desiccated spruce planking stripped from the
ceiling of the mess; needless to say, these boards were not
particularly strong or flexible. Most of the ribs were fabri-

cated from old barrel staves, so each frame had to be wrapped with twine to prevent the wood from splintering.

The sledges had even less to recommend them. For runners we used brittle birch boards scavenged from a battered mess table. Many of these pieces shattered at our first attempts to bend them into the proper shape, forcing us to fabricate some of the runners from ash oars. On several occasions the inferior materials made available to us by Brusilov caused me to quarrel so violently with him that I still cringe to think about it. He was convinced that all we would have to do was to set off on some heading—a difficult journey to be sure, but a short one—and very soon we would reach Franz Josef Land, after five or six days at the most. So he smiled indulgently at our efforts to make the sledges and kayaks as sturdy as possible. He claimed it would be far wiser to use one of the ship's lifeboats, and reminded us of Lieutenant De Long's expedition.* But I did not view our journey so optimistically, and the rigors of fate would soon reveal that our trek across the ice—which I had estimated would take a month—would in fact turn out to be even more terrible than I imagined. It would have been impossible to haul a heavy lifeboat mounted on a sledge and laden with 2,400 pounds of supplies over the rugged pack ice.

In any case we did not even have an accurate fix on our present position, or know whether we would find land at all, as we did not possess a map of Franz Josef Land. To be able to trace our perambulations over the ice, I painstakingly drew a grid of meridians and parallels onto which

* George Washington De Long was captain of the *Jeannette* (see Introduction). After his ship was crushed, De Long and his crew set out across the ice with three of the *Jeannette*'s lifeboats.

I copied an enlarged outline of Franz Josef Land as it appeared on the map in Nansen's *Farthest North*. Nansen himself said that he ascribed no particular accuracy to this map and had only included it in order to give an approximate idea of the archipelago. It showed Cape Fligely at 82°12′ north and, to the north, the great expanse of Petermann Land with King Oscar Land to the northwest. How surprised we were in early March and April, therefore, when our astronomical observations pinpointed our position in the middle of these landmasses, while in reality there was nothing but endless pack ice as far as the eye could see.* There were no signs of any nearby land—nor any polar bears (the previous year at the same time we had shot forty-seven), nor leads in the ice, nor the dark line of a "water sky"† along the horizon that is normally an indication of open water. On the contrary, the flat horizon stretched into the distance in all directions, dashing all our hopeful fantasies. These unmistakable signs foretold a long and arduous route through deep snow and over treacherous ice.

It is true that in January, when the noonday sky began to glow with a faint rosy hue, some of us, including myself, saw something in the far distance that stood out like land against this pinkish background, but it remained visible for only a few hours. Then, the colorful glow sud-

---

* Petermann Land and King Oscar Land had been reported by an Austrian expedition in 1873, whose crew claimed to have seen the distant islands far to the north of the northernmost point of Franz Josef Land. Both landmasses turned out to be mirages. Albanov's failure to find these lands would prove a crucial step in debunking them.

† The sky takes on a different color when it is reflecting open water rather than ice.

denly faded into darkness, and a pack of white foxes trotted by, not far from the ship. Perhaps it was Cape Fligely or Prince Rudolf Island that we had seen. Since then, however, many months have gone by, and we have had no additional sightings of land. Whether the land we saw was real or imagined, since then we have been drifting ever farther away from it, on a relentless northerly course.

On clear sunny days, prompted by the vague hope of discovering a distant landmass, I often climbed up the mainmast to the crow's nest, about eighty feet above sea level. I searched the horizon in vain. I could see nothing but a rugged expanse of ice, which toward the south, in the direction of our goal, took the shape of an immense, impassable barrier. It seemed to block the way to freedom for our sledges, which, in aggregate, would be heavily loaded with over 2,400 pounds. But it was certainly only an illusion: We always found a passage, although we had yet to discover the superhuman effort it would require. At that point in time we still imagined that we would cover at least seven miles a day.

———

When the sun was shining, it was exhilarating to be up there in the crow's nest, with only the slightest breeze stirring in the ice-covered rigging. The *Saint Anna* seemed to be dreaming under her sparkling white carapace, as if a masterly hand had adorned her with exquisite crystals of hoarfrost and robed her hull in snowflakes. From time to time garlands of snow would come loose from the rigging and drop softly like flowers onto the dormant ship, which looks narrower and longer from aloft. The slender, towering yards seem elegant, almost fragile. Bathed in dazzling rays of light, the tackle throws a magical reflection onto the slumbering vessel, motionless in her icy prison for now a year and a half. What will be her fate? How long will it be before she stirs on her frozen bed—this ice floe from the Kara Sea that trapped her off the coast of the Yamal Peninsula? Will it be somewhere between Svalbard and Greenland, far from her current prison? And when she finally awakens, will she then glide unhindered into her own element, hoist her greatsails, and turn away from the realm of "white death" toward the sunlit blue waters of the south, where her wounds will heal, and everything she has suffered will seem like a terrible dream?

Or during a bitter night, when the snow is whipped through the sky by the storm, and the moon and stars are engulfed by a fearful blackness, will she be rudely awakened in the midst of the tempest by the splintering of spars and the cracking of planks, heralding her annihilation? The hull, then, will shudder in agony and her wooden sides will shatter. After some time only heaps of debris and a new mound of ice will mark her grave. The storm will sing her eulogy and strew the site of the disaster with fresh snow. And by the nearest pressure ridge a handful of desperate men will try to save what they can of their belongings in the dark, still clinging to life, still hoping to escape death.

What is your destiny, proud ship? Your slow destruction has already begun, although even the smallest planks have never been torn willingly from your hull. But the men you have carried this far are struggling, like you, filled with a desperate courage inspired by the treachery of the elements. Their only concern is how to stretch their supplies as long as possible.

Already the second hard winter on the ice has passed. Endless polar nights and their terrifying darkness are giving way to the first timid rays of a triumphant sun, which traces an ever-higher arc each day, awakening life all around us. The crew has also come back to life. From morning 'til night men bustle about carrying myriad tools as they swarm to and fro between the ship and a fleet of strange craft lined up on the ice nearby. Each of these odd vessels consists of a long sledge set on high trestles, with a light sailcloth kayak placed on soft cushions between the rails of the sledge, as if resting in a shallow basket. With their bows and sterns jutting well beyond the lengths of the sledges that bear them, and wearing fresh coats of black paint, the kayaks look quite formidable. This somber impression is brightened somewhat by the wide strips of white canvas that attach each kayak firmly to the body of its sledge so that they form a single craft. Ropes run diagonally from one strip of canvas to the next over the kayaks, which help secure the boats to the sledges, and also protect them against jagged blocks of ice.

On board ship and all around is a hive of industry. The final preparations for our departure are being tended to; those who are staying behind are eager to help. Everyone has a great deal to do. Those who are craftsmen by trade make use of their skills; others lend a hand by stowing baggage and supplies. Denisov, our wonderful harpooner, is rushing around more than anybody, even though he is among those who will be staying behind. The only ones absent are Lieutenant Brusilov, Miss Zhdanko, and the harpooner Shlensky, all of whom, for over a week now from morning until night, have been writing the letters we shall deliver to people who live in the present—unlike those of us on the ship, who live only in the past and the future, awaiting our deliverance from the polar ice.

There was little variety in our provisions. The ship's biscuits, before they were packed, were thoroughly dried, then placed in twenty-pound sacks and hermetically sewn closed. We took one of the three tents included in the *Saint Anna's* inventory. It was large, round, and—compared with Nansen's—very heavy (about sixty pounds). Later, when it became wet and frozen, it was too awkward to carry and we had to leave it behind. But during the first half of our journey by sledge we were very glad to have its protection against the cold and snowstorms. By way of firearms, we carried two repeating rifles, three seal-hunting rifles, and one double-barreled shotgun, with about 120 pounds of ammunition. In addition to all this we had two harpoons, the usual warm clothing, instruments and equipment such as axes, skis, dishes, all sorts of repair material, and so on. Over and above the actual weight of the kayaks and sledges, we had to haul about 2,600 pounds.

To start with, two men were assigned to pull each kayak/sledge combination. Each of us had a sailcloth hauling strap to which a rope was fastened. The strap was worn over one shoulder and across the chest, and the end of the rope was fastened to one of the forward uprights of the sledge, allowing the man pulling to steady the bow of the attached kayak with one hand and thereby steer the sledge where he wanted, while he held a ski pole in the other. There was one man on each side of the sledge, which would have made it easy to pull, had the route not been blocked at every step by ice hummocks, and had we not been constantly sinking into the snow up to our knees.

Alas, we soon had to face the fact that it was practically impossible for only two men to pull each sledge.

I have already mentioned that there were no maps on board that were of any use to us, and that I had copied our only existing map out of Nansen's book. Other than that volume and Kolchak's* *The Ice of the Siberian Sea,* we had no other relevant works. Although Lieutenant Brusilov had bought a small library for hundreds of rubles before our departure, it contained only novels, stories, and old journals—not a single book of any use to us except Nansen's *Farthest North.* Nansen was our only guide, and provided everything we knew about Franz Josef Land. For example, almost twenty years earlier (1895 to 1896), Nansen and Johansen had crossed the archipelago and wintered in a gloomy hut at a place they christened Jackson Island. The following year, on Northbrook Island near Cape Flora, they met up with Jackson himself,† who had spent several winters there. A small group of buildings had been erected. Perhaps they were still standing, with their store of supplies? Who could say? All we knew was that Nansen spoke highly of the hunting at Cape Flora and Franz Josef Land, and we counted on finding walruses there that we could take by surprise while they slept, and shoot without danger. Drawing all our knowledge from Nansen's experiences, we treated his book like a precious treasure. I had reread it so often that I could cite entire passages from memory. I had

---

* Aleksandr Vasilyevich Kolchak: Arctic explorer and naval officer who was recognized from 1919 to 1920 by the "Whites" as supreme ruler of Russia; after his downfall he was put to death by the Bolsheviks.

† Frederick Jackson's expedition on board the *Windward* took place from 1894 to 1897.

noted all the details in my notebook, particularly those which could help me out of a tight spot, if need be. But what purpose would all this information serve if we could not find this unknown land? I had also copied down the altitude of the sun and astronomy charts for the coming year and a half. I had found these figures in an English technical journal I had come across by chance in the ship's supplies, along with a stock of old marine charts and logbooks, dating from the purchase of the *Saint Anna*.

From Franz Josef Land we would still have to reach Svalbard, and we knew even less about that archipelago.* In the same English journal, I found quite by chance ten or twelve navigational coordinates that approximately matched the latitude and longitude of Svalbard. I copied these coordinates onto a chart that I had sketched with meridians and parallels, but I had no idea what they might mean. Did they indicate an island, a cape, a mountain, or a bay? In short, they were on my chart, and my imagination could draw totally arbitrary lines to link them all together.

We also knew, regarding Franz Josef Land, that the *Stella Polare*, belonging to the Duke of Abruzzi, had sailed through the British Channel as far as the Bay of Teplitz, and that in 1912 the Russian lieutenant Sedov had intended to disembark on one of the islands. After sending his ship back to Arkhangel'sk, Sedov had planned to spend the winter there before attempting to reach the North Pole the following spring.

On the eve of our departure Brusilov summoned me to read the draft of an order he wanted to copy and give to

---

* Albanov could not count on being rescued from rarely visited Franz Josef Land. Svalbard, however, was a regular stop for exploring and hunting expeditions.

me. This document, dated April 10, ordered us to set out right away, with our homemade boats and sledges, carrying provisions for two months, on a journey which we would pursue until we reached land. Then, depending on circumstances, we were to try to reach the British Channel and Cape Flora, where we would be sure to find some huts and winter stores. Temperatures permitting, we were then to head for Svalbard, but without losing sight of the coast of Franz Josef Land. To the extreme south of the archipelago we might come across inhabitants and, offshore, perhaps some seal hunters. These were the directives, so to speak, for our southward trek. At the same time, the document set out the up-to-date calculation of the wages owed to each of us by the owner of the *Saint Anna*, Boris Alexeyevich Brusilov,* a retired general and landowner in Moscow, who had financed the expedition. Our signatures confirmed that the amount was correct.

Late in the evening the lieutenant called me once more into his cabin to give me a list of items we would be taking with us and which I must, if possible, return to him at a later date. Here is that list as it was entered into the ship's record: 2 Remington rifles, 1 Norwegian hunting rifle, 1 double-barreled shotgun, 2 repeating rifles, 1 ship's log transformed into a pedometer for measuring distances covered, 2 harpoons, 2 axes, 1 saw, 2 compasses, 14 pairs of skis, 1 first-quality malitsa, 12 second-quality malitsi,† 1 sleep-

* Lieutenant Brusilov's uncle.
† Malitsi are heavy, sacklike, Samoyed garments sewn from reindeer hide, with the fur on the inside. Slipped over the head, they have crude openings to accommodate the arms and the face. Thirteen of the men in Albanov's party used malitsi in lieu of sleeping bags at night.

ing bag, 1 chronometer, 1 sextant, 14 rucksacks, and 1 small pair of binoculars.

Brusilov asked me if he had forgotten to list anything. His pettiness astounded me. It was as if he thought there were horses waiting at the gangway to take those of us who would be leaving to the nearest railway station or steamship terminal. Had the lieutenant forgotten that we were about to set off on foot on a daunting trek across drifting ice, in order to search for an unknown landmass, and this under worse conditions than any men who had gone before us? Did he have no greater concerns on this last evening than toting up rucksacks, axes, a defective ship's log, a saw, and harpoons? If truth be told, even as he read the list to me, I felt myself succumbing to a familiar rage. I experienced the sensation of strangling as my throat constricted in anger. But I controlled myself and reminded Brusilov that he had forgotten to list the tent, the kayaks, the sledges, a mug, cups, and a galvanized bucket. He immediately wrote down the tent, but decided not to mention the dishes. "I will not list the kayaks or sledges, either," he offered. "In all probability they will be badly damaged by the end of your trip, and the freight to ship them from Svalbard would cost more than they are worth. But if you succeed in getting them to Alexandrovsk, deliver them to the local police for safekeeping." I told Brusilov I was in agreement with this.

I left the lieutenant's cabin very upset, and went below. On the way to my cabin, Denisov stopped me to ask where I would open the packet of ship's mail and post the letters—in Norway or Russia? That was the last straw, and I could not contain my emotions any longer. I exploded and threatened to dump not only the mail, but also the rucksacks, the cups, and the mugs into the first open lead we came to, because I had serious doubts that we would ever reach a mail train in Norway, Russia, or anywhere else. But then I quickly regained my composure and promised Denisov that, wherever we landed, I would make every effort to see that the ship's mail reached its destination.

Denisov went on his way, reassured. The ship was dark. Everyone had gone to bed. I was dismayed and depressed. It was as if I were already wandering across the endless, icy wastes, without any hope of returning to the ship, and with only the unknown lying ahead.

On that gloomy, decisive night prior to my departure from the *Saint Anna,* filled with anxiety, I wondered about each of the men who would be accompanying me. I already possessed grave doubts about their health and stamina. One was fifty-six years old and all of them complained of sore feet; not one of them was really fit. One man had open sores on his legs, another had a hernia, a third had been suffering from pains in his chest for a long time, and all, without exception, had asthma and palpitations.

In short, these were the dark thoughts that assailed and disheartened me that evening. Was this a premonition of some great misfortune that I was heading for, with no hope of escape?

Last Day on Board
the *Saint Anna*

When the long-awaited day finally arrived, and only a few hours remained before our departure, a slight regret came to trouble my thoughts: I was leaving behind the ship and its crew. Now they would be left to themselves and to the vagaries of an uncertain fate. I had become very fond of the *Saint Anna* during our long voyage; so often, in dangerous situations, she had provided us with shelter and safety. And had I not also enjoyed pleasant experiences here, particularly at the beginning of our journey? At that time we lived in complete harmony and knew how to put up a good front even at difficult moments, accepting misfortune cheerfully and bravely. We had spent many lively evenings together playing dominoes in the pleasant saloon, by the ruddy light of a good fire. Water would bubble in the samovar, ready for tea. There was kerosene to spare then, and our lamps gave enough light for any activity. The men were in high spirits, and enlivened the conversation with all sorts of amusing stories; everyone freely voiced his expectations about the future. Good humor reigned.

When we embarked on our voyage, most mariners and oceanographers familiar with the Arctic were of the opinion that the ice in the southern reaches of the Kara Sea was not subject to the general movements of the polar ice pack. Once we became icebound, we thought the *Saint Anna* would drift to and fro a little, but that we would remain in these southerly waters until the spring thaw set us free and opened up the mouth of the Yenisei River. From there, Brusilov planned to travel upriver to Krasnoyarsk in order to purchase fresh supplies and fetch the mail. At the same time, we would stock up on coal and fit out the ship so that we could continue on our way. The *Saint Anna* seemed certain to withstand the difficult ordeal ahead, for she was in every way superior to the two Norwegian ships, *Nimrod* and *Saint Foka*, that had initially been equipped for seal hunting and later bought for the purpose of expeditions. The cabins were a little chilly on our ship, to be sure, but we would soon take care of this inconvenience.

While we were taking on more coal at Dikson Island, Brusilov would go directly to Krasnoyarsk in the motor launch so that he would not have to wait for the regularly scheduled steamer, and thus gain more time. In this way we hoped eventually to reach Vladivostok, even if it took a year. What did it matter! A hunting expedition must primarily pursue its hunting objectives, and this we would do since the sea to the north of Siberia was teeming with walruses. Those were the plans we discussed every evening around the samovar as we drank our tea. Miss Yerminiya

Zhdanko played the role of the perfect hostess, and showed a lively interest in our projects. She never blamed us for getting her into "an unholy mess," as we were in the habit of saying; in fact she would get quite annoyed when we said this, for she shared all our problems with extraordinary courage. At first the role of hostess often proved terribly embarrassing for Miss Zhdanko. If someone so much as asked her to pour the tea, she would instantly blush to the roots of her hair, mortified that she had not first suggested it herself. This charming trait provoked much teasing from others on board the ship. For instance, when Brusilov wanted tea, he would first hold his breath for a while, trying to make it look like he was blushing. After this effort had caused his face to turn thoroughly red, he would shyly turn to Miss Zhdanko and say, "Lady of the house, please be so good as to pour me a glass of tea." At the sight of the lieutenant's shy, blushing countenance, she would immediately blush furiously herself, prompting everybody to laugh and shout, "She's on fire!" and inspiring someone to run for water.

But those happier times—in the first half of the first winter, now in the distant past—occurred before we had begun to drift northward. The *Saint Anna* was then as trim and shipshape as she had been in the harbor on the Neva in St. Petersburg, near the Nicholas Bridge, and interested people were being invited to take a little trip along the coast in "Nordenskiöld's* footsteps." The white paint was still fresh on her hull and decks, the mahogany furnishings in

---

* The great Swedish explorer, Baron Nils Adolf Erik Nordenskiöld, had made the first and by 1912 the only traverse of the Northeast Passage in 1878–79. See Introduction.

the saloon gleamed like mirrors, magnificent carpets covered the floors. The hold and storeroom were overflowing with supplies and every delicacy that might tempt the palate. But these irreplaceable luxuries had disappeared at an alarming rate. We were soon forced to nail boards over the skylights and portholes, and pull our bunks away from the hull, so that our pillows and blankets did not freeze to the walls at night. We also had to cover the ceilings and floors with boards, sailcloth, layers of cardboard and felt, and finally hang small basins in numerous places to catch the water that dripped incessantly from the ceilings and walls. Our kerosene had all been burned, and for a long time we had been using lamps fashioned from tin cans containing a mixture of bear fat and seal blubber, the wicks of which gave off more smoke than light. In winter, the temperature belowdecks hovered between 28° and 23° Fahrenheit, and the "smoke pots" scarcely brightened the dense gloom. Several of these lamps placed on a table gave only a faint circle of light: Their tiny, trembling flames cast a vague reddish glow, and this dim lighting gave those around the table a shadowy, spectral look—the one and only advantage of these "smoke pots," since our faces were as filthy as our worn clothing. Our soap had been used up long ago, and our attempts to manufacture some had failed miserably: It stuck to one's face like a greasy glue and was nearly impossible to wash off. Our poor Miss Zhdanko! Now if she blushed, one would not even notice it beneath the layer of soot covering her face. In the saloon, the walls and ceiling were covered with a crust of ice. The layer grew thinner near the center of the room, which remained virtually the only place where it could not form. The ever-trickling water had taken the varnish off the wood, and it now hung from the walls in long, dirty, water-sodden strips. Wherever the woodwork had been stripped and saturated with humidity, mildew and mold were rampant.

But necessity accustoms one to many forms of ugliness, and we were no exception. The changes occurred gradually, and we had time to get used to these sordid surroundings; in the end, we no longer noticed the squalor of our living quarters, as the degradation was spread over a period of eighteen months, and our pathetic lamps masked its hideousness.

And yet despite such wretchedness, I awoke on the last morning filled with melancholy at the prospect of leaving the *Saint Anna*. What memories haunted me! I had spent a whole year and a half of my life in this tiny, cramped cabin, which now, in recent days especially, had become my pleasant retreat. I led my own life here. The sounds of my companions, who spent their days on the other side of the bulkhead, reached me from time to time, while nothing of my solitude filtered through to them. The walls of my cabin enclosed my thoughts and plans, my hopes and fears; they were mine alone.

Our departure was set for the evening of April 10. I went up on deck. The weather was fine. An unusually clear sky stretched as far as the distant, unchanging horizon; it was the first true spring day of the year. The air was pure and still, without the slightest breeze, and there was not a cloud in the sky. The sun cast its warming rays; it had even begun to melt the snow on the dark canvas hulls of our kayaks. With the help of the harpooner Denisov, I calculated the angle of the sun with my sextant and chronometer. At noon I obtained a favorable enough longitude reading to be able to determine our position at 82°58.5′ north and 60°5′ east of Greenwich. In the meantime, my companions moved all our kayaks and sledges to the starboard side of the ship and lined them up near the gangway, their bows facing south. My sledge was at the head of the row.

The farewell dinner was held at three that afternoon, and was probably the inspiration of our steward Regald and Kalmikov the cook, our indefatigable "singer and poet." He had been laboring in the galley since dawn in service to his art, and had even gone so far as to put aside his notebook of poetry, something he rarely let out of his sight. The steward in the meantime prepared one of the rooms belowdecks, pulling together the benches, setting the table, and doing his utmost to make it a real gala dinner. In their cabins above, crewmembers hurriedly finished their letters; for several days now, those who were staying behind had been constantly writing.

At the appointed hour, we all sat down at the mess table for dinner. I, who usually sat apart, took my place among my companions. The captain was slightly delayed by something; he would appear shortly. A dark mood filled the room, although everyone tried to look cheerful. But the jokes and forced laughter could not conceal the pervasive sadness and anxiety, among both those who were leaving and those who were staying. Some of those who were to remain on the ship expressed concern that each of the sledges—laden with nearly 400 pounds—was too heavy to be hauled by just two men over such rough terrain, but those who were leaving affected an air of confidence. Then it was decided that everyone on board would help haul the sledges as far as our first camp. Each of those who would be staying behind assigned himself to the sledge of whoever was his closest companion.

Physical strength had nothing to do with the makeup of each hauling team; it was based solely on the bonds of friendship. Those of us who were leaving bragged about the special attributes of our personal "tugboats" who were to haul us out of the "quiet harbor into the open sea" on the initial leg of our journey.

"Just look at that grinning mug!" someone declared of his escort. "He'll really put his back into it!" My own "tugboat" was the harpooner Denisov, and his robust physique apparently provoked envy among some of my companions, although they pretended to be indifferent.

As we gathered around the table, the gramophone provided background music, including what had lately been our two favorite recordings: "Come Ashore," and "The Call of the Snow-white Gull." These songs had been played several hundred times during our four-day Easter celebration, so every chord was familiar—indeed, we were all rather sick of them, but they evoked pleasant memories of the early months of our voyage, when we were filled with high hopes as we sailed along the Norwegian coast. This confidence had sustained us for a long while, even when the ice had closed in around us. In those halycon days our cook/poet, Kalmikov, had composed a long poem, put it to music, and sung it to us for hours on end. I have forgotten the bulk of it, alas, but I still remember these confident lines:

Under the flag of Mother Russia
Our captain will show us the way
Along the coast of Siberia
In our ship so fine and gay.

Finally Lieutenant Brusilov came below and the meal began. Miss Zhdanko served the soup and encouraged us to eat heartily. We were very hungry, since it was already four o'clock and normally we ate at noon. In spite of our limited supplies, the meal looked like a banquet. But would we ever enjoy sitting down together like this again? And if indeed one day we did, how many of us would be there? Although no one spoke of it, we must have all been thinking the same thing, for the table was uncharacteristically silent; joy was not one of the guests.

It seemed as if we were fulfilling one final, painful obligation.

After I left the table, I went up on deck to shoot a final sun sight with the sextant. The sun was setting in a reddish smear, and the horizon was veiled in mist—indications of an imminent change in the weather. I marked our position on the chart, and carried it back to my sledge with the sextant and the chronometer. I had put on a double layer of underclothing in addition to my normal clothes and had given everything else to those staying behind. There was only one personal item I was taking with me: an icon of Saint Nicholas the Miracle-worker.

Soon my cabin was empty: I cast a farewell glance round the bare little room and then went out onto the ice. Our traveling outfits consisted of high boots in leather or sealskin, with uppers made of the same sailcloth we had used for our jackets and trousers; we had warm undergarments, a cap, and earmuffs. We made a strange-looking group, all kitted out with our towlines over our shoulders and a long ski pole in one hand. My comrades were lined up, facing south. The dark hulls of the kayaks with their high, raked bows and white canvas lashing strips were reminiscent of a flock of wild ducks that had gathered to fly south to warmer lands. Unfortunately, however, they could not fly and we would have to haul them.

The sledges had been packed with all our personal belongings underneath, and on top of them all the oars, skis, hides, firearms, tent, etc. They were very heavy, too heavy for their narrow runners, which sank deep into the snow. Denisov had made a trial run with each of the sleds and was not very happy with the result. But there was no point in delaying the departure now. I could not bring myself to leave anything behind, since after careful reckoning I had chosen only basic necessities. If need be, we could offload along the way.

When it was time to leave, everyone was there, without exception, to walk with us some of the way, including our dog, Ulka, the last survivor of the six hounds Brusilov had brought from his uncle's estate. Finally, even the lieutenant himself came out and stood behind my sledge to help me push it.

Everyone seemed to be waiting for a signal, so I took off my cap and made the sign of the cross. They all did the same, then someone shouted, Hurrah! We all repeated the cry in unison, leaned into our hauling straps, and at that moment our sledges began to move toward the south.

The closest accessible land, Cape Fligely, on Prince Rudolf Island, was sixty-five nautical miles to the south-southwest. But we would never catch sight of it, because we would be pushed irresistibly northward by the drifting ice pack, even as we trudged laboriously to the south.

Over the Polar Ice Pack

With the runners creaking and pitching like boats plying ocean swells, our sledges moved southward over the ice. We could see that ice hummocks and pressure ridges lay ahead of us, but we were confident there was a passage between them.

Although the route was quite straightforward at the start, and each sledge was being hauled by at least three men (two of them by four men), we did not seem to be making much headway. After half an hour, we made a short stop and discovered that we were still quite close to the *Saint Anna*.

No sooner had we climbed up one of the first pressure ridges than the runners broke on one of the sledges. We repaired the damage at once and set off again after three quarters of an hour. Brusilov, who was very concerned about this accident, immediately sent two men back to the ship to fetch two parrels* from the mizzenmast, in

---

* A parrel is a wooden sleeve that slides up and down a ship's mast, connecting a yard or other spar to the mast.

case we had to make other repairs in the future. Behind a high rise that hid the ship from view, Miss Zhdanko and Kalmikov, the cook, decided to return to the ship. The weather was rapidly deteriorating. Two hours later a strong south-southwesterly gale began to blow, bringing with it a raging snowstorm.

We pitched camp for the night. The tent was placed in the center with the kayaks propped up all around it for protection. Our pedometer indicated that we had barely covered three miles. Soon we were all gathered together in the tent around our blubber stove, drinking milky tea. To everyone's surprise, Brusilov handed out pieces of chocolate, and even produced a bottle of champagne. Although we had only one mouthful each, it was not the quantity that mattered, but the fact that we were at 83° latitude, toasting our respective homeward journeys! We chatted for a while about the past, the present, and the future, and then bade a moving farewell to our helpful companions, who set off for the ship on their skis.

The blizzard gained in strength, causing the tent to snap and groan. Exhausted, we slid into our malitsi and immediately fell into a deep, comforting sleep. When we awoke at ten o'clock to the sound of the gale still howling with the same force, we could not imagine traveling on in such conditions. Flurries of snow had been blown into the tent, and our furs were dusted with white. It was a bad start, and most discouraging. The thermometer indicated −9° Fahrenheit. But we had to think about maintaining our strength, so we got up to prepare a meal. We had enormous difficulty in opening the tent door, and even more so in uncovering the kayaks buried in the snow. We eventually managed to boil some water for tea, and to warm up some cans of Australian meat, which dulled our hunger. We then climbed back into our malitsi, since the dreadful weather precluded any other form of activity, and that is how we spent the day.

The next day brought no improvement, and in the end we were stopped for three whole days. We stayed in the tent the entire time, bundled up in our reindeer hides, eating and sleeping. My companions preferred sleeping in pairs: They would slip their legs and the lower parts of their bodies into one malitsa, and pull the other malitsa over their heads. This method is recommended for creating and preserving body heat, but it has the disadvantage of disturbing one's sleep each time the other sleeper moves or turns over. For that reason, I always preferred to sleep alone, and later developments would show how right I was. Bed companions often squabbled, which occasionally led to more serious arguments. Generally, the disruptive partner did not even realize how much he had been disturbing his neighbor, and felt that all forthcoming complaints were totally unjustified. Insults would be exchanged, occasionally degenerating into prodding and shoving or half-hearted punches, until eventually the adversaries turned their backs on each other and endeavored to fall asleep again. In most cases, that is how hostilities ended. The most quarrelsome bed-partners were the inseparable friends, Konrad and Shpakovsky.

Those who chose to sleep alone had to accept a certain heat loss because it was impossible to fit one's entire body into one's malitsa. I tried to ward off the worst of the cold by jamming my legs as deeply as possible into my malitsa while covering my head and chest with my warm jacket.

And this is how we stayed for three days and three nights, immobile. Since it was impossible to move on, we had to resign ourselves to the inevitable. At least it gave us a good opportunity to become accustomed to life in the tent, and physically we were quite comfortable. At times some of the group would sing to try to brighten our solitude, or to drown out the howling of the storm. Only one of them, old Anisimov, who back on board used to complain of pains in his back and legs, was becoming more and more listless, so I decided to send him back to the *Saint Anna*. It was the only solution, as we would not be able to nurse him later on, and he was no longer fit enough to pull a sledge.

On the evening of the thirteenth the wind had abated a little and suddenly we were awakened by noises and shouts from outside the tent. When we opened up the entry flap we were greeted enthusiastically by three messengers from the *Saint Anna:* Denisov, Melbart, and Regald. They had wanted to come and visit us the night before, but the blizzard had prevented them from doing so. Today they had braved the elements in order to bring us some hot soup, which we gulped down ravenously. They told us that the ship was buried in snow up to the gunwales. They brought us some shovels, and we immediately started digging the kayaks out from beneath the snow. Our faithful friends left again that evening with our ailing comrade, but the next day one of them, Regald, returned with his belongings to take Anisimov's place.

At around noon, I took another sun sight and was very surprised to find a latitude reading of 83°17'. I was wondering about the precision of my calculations, when Regald handed me a letter from the lieutenant, confirming that he had found a latitude of 83°18' that same morning. In that case there could be no doubt: In the course of the last four days the storm had driven us northward by roughly twenty-two miles. On our first day's trek we had covered only three miles, which meant that so far, in spite of all our efforts, we were actually nineteen miles farther from our goal than when we had left the ship! This observation immediately drained me of almost all hope. But then the thought that summer was on its way—and that northerly winds would prevail throughout most of the season—restored my courage and convinced me to carry on. So we made ready, packed up the tent, and set off. Then a new, disturbing incident occurred: We had hardly gone a few yards before we were overcome by dizziness and felt so weak that we had to lie down.

Had the three days of sleep done us more harm than good, or were we already so worn out by the most recent Arctic winter that our strength was nearly gone? I looked at each of my companions: They all had wan, yellowish complexions which stood out in the bright sunlight with frightening clarity—something we had not noticed in the winter twilight, particularly in the dim light of the blubber lamps.

After a while, we felt better, but rather embarrassed by our weakness. We set out with only three of the seven kayaks to begin with, which we hauled two miles to the south, and then returned to fetch the other four. The *Saint Anna* stood out clearly over the pack ice, the weather was fine, and the sun felt warm already. These things combined to restore both our courage and our undaunted determination to overcome every obstacle, and to attain our goal, however long it might take us.

That day we traveled nearly four miles and camped in a place sheltered by high mounds of ice. The following day was the same. We did three stages at this speed. Our route was so encumbered with obstacles and so obstructed by ice, which had piled up in many places to form formidable pressure ridges, that it was impossible to go any faster. To make things even worse, it was becoming increasingly clear that the runners of our sleds were too narrow and too close together: They sank deep into the snow, and we wasted all our time and energy in dragging them free. We logged only two and a half miles that day. The two crewmembers who had come earlier, Denisov and Melbart, joined us again with unfailing devotion, bringing us more hot soup. They made fun of our snail's pace and threatened to come and visit us daily for another full week. Denisov, especially, who was half Ukrainian and half Norwegian, showed great interest in our exploit; he was very fit and had much Arctic experience, and could travel up to forty miles a day on his skis. Without a doubt he was the most capable of all those who had remained on board, and since he had an unusual background I will tell you a little about him.

He left his father's home in the Ukraine when he was thirteen, stowed away in the hold of a large steamship, and on disembarking in a foreign port he found employment as a sailor, working different ships until one day he ended up on South Georgia Island, in the stormy waters off Antarctica. There he went to work on a whaler and learned to become a harpooner. He later married a Norwegian girl and was just as happy in Norway as he had been in the Ukraine, or so he used to say. When he heard of Brusilov's intention to go whale hunting in the Arctic and Far East, he volunteered at once, although he could have obtained a better-paid position in Norway. But the special nature of this new expedition appealed to his adventurous spirit. Although Denisov felt entirely at home in Norway, he loved Russia passionately, and it had always been his cherished dream to sail aboard a Russian whaler.

By April 16, we had lost all communication with the *Saint Anna.* Denisov could no longer catch up with us, and by evening the vessel had disappeared beneath the horizon. Yet we were gradually getting used to this nomadic existence. We got up at seven in the morning and prepared our breakfast. During the early days, we still had a little bit of seal blubber to cook our meals and melt snow for drinking water. Our stove was a very primitive and inefficient arrangement: We had simply jammed a zinc bucket with its lid well down into an iron, boxlike container, and beneath the bucket sat an iron pan containing the blubber we burned for fuel. When the apparatus was lit, the temperature rose inside the tent, but there was so much smoke that we soon looked like gypsies. Later, our skin would become even darker.

As a rule, we set off at around nine o'clock with a few sledges, which we pulled for about two hours, and then returned for the others. It was always a very tiring ordeal, and every day we regretted the fact that our sledges were not fitted with wider runners. The snow was very deep and we would sink to our knees. It was impossible to haul the heavy sledges on skis, since they would simply slide backward. After this exhausting chore, we would sit in the shelter of our kayaks and nibble on biscuits with a bit of chocolate. We had to be sparing with our meager provisions. After resting for an hour and a half, we would haul the first three sledges and kayaks, one of which contained the tent, for another mile or two, until we reached a suitable camping spot. We always chose the highest hummock of ice we could find so that we would have an uninterrupted view of the horizon. Two men would stay and keep watch over the tent while all the others went back for the remaining sledges and kayaks. We lined the floor of the tent with covers and coats as well as the sailcloth that normally lashed the kayaks to the sledges. As I have previously mentioned, the kayaks were placed in a circle around the tent, together with the sledges, which we attached with ropes to the ends of the tent guy lines. By seven in the evening, we were all settled into the tent, our legs tucked deep into our malitsi while we waited for our improvised stove to heat the water for our evening tea. To save blubber, we rarely let the water come to a boil, and were quite happy with just a warm drink. Then we would lace up the entrance to the tent, already filled with smoke and steam. The evening meal—consisting of tea, biscuits, and canned meat—helped us to forget the cold and our fatigue. When our supply of Australian cans ran out, we turned to Skorikov's "bouillon," which had been prepared with granules of dried meat. We improved the taste of the broth by adding a dried vegetable. These evening hours in the tent were far and away the most pleasant of the day, and did not fail to revive our flagging spirits, although our conversation always turned to the same burning questions: When would we find land? And from there would we manage to reach Cape Flora? What would happen after that, and would we ever see our homes again?

We took off our snow-sodden boots and hung them to dry outside on our ski poles. Generally by morning they had dried in the wind. It was also in the evening that I wrote up my diary and made my calculations of the day's navigational observations. When we ran out of fuel, however, the hours spent in the tent became almost unbearable. Those bitter evenings were very silent. We sat hunched together, gloomy and taciturn, huddled deep inside our reindeer hides in our respective corners. No welcoming tea to warm us; our miserable supper was made up of dried biscuit and ice shards melted in the mouth. With the biscuit we were allowed a spoonful of butter that was still so frozen it was hardly a substitute for hot food. Nor was the ice a suitable replacement for the tea, since it did not even manage to quench our raging thirst. Some of the men, later on, managed to get used to drinking seawater, in which they would dunk the ship's biscuit to make a broth flavored with dried onion. There, too, cruel necessity proved to be an effective taskmaster: Those who could stand to drink salt water found that it very quickly lost its bitter taste. For cooking soups, we generally used seawater diluted with some ice.

During the first third of our odyssey, we had to put up with many of these cold evenings, because at that time we rarely came across any open water, and consequently no seals or polar bears. Without a doubt the most unpleasant moment was getting up in the morning. We had to leave our warm malitsi and face the biting cold without a warm drink in our stomachs. Breakfast would consist of nothing more than a hard biscuit. We wore our malitsi to take down the tent and pack up our belongings, but finally we had to remove them and the hard work of hauling the sledges began. In dark, frigid weather with snow whirling in all directions, our spirits were as bleak as our surroundings. It seemed as if our route would never lead us to a more hospitable place, and that the dreadful blizzard would never yield to milder climes.

Toward the eleventh day, when we had traveled roughly twenty-eight miles from the *Saint Anna,* three sailors came to see me and admitted they could not go on. They requested permission to return to the ship, believing that if they continued they would surely perish. I had the impression that these three fellows, to be honest, were among the strongest in our group, but perhaps they had expected to see land after five or six days, and to be rescued ten days afterward at the latest. Disappointed by the present situation, they now wished to return to the ship, where they would suffer neither cold nor hunger. As all of them had followed me of their own free will, and since I hardly considered our situation to be enviable, I felt I had no choice but to accept their request. If they were going to be discouraged so quickly, they were hardly of much use to me. As the weather moreover had been quite reasonable over the last few days, with no snow flurries, I was convinced that by following our tracks the three men would easily find their way back. I let them go. They refused to take any of the heavy kayak/sledge combinations they had been hauling with us. They left on skis, warmly dressed, carrying big rucksacks filled with biscuits; they also had a rifle with ammunition. I estimated they would reach the ship by the following day. But I waited for twenty-four hours at our present campsite in case they needed to return. During our enforced rest period, we dismantled two of the now useless sledges and kayaks for firewood. I had also given the three "fair-weather friends" a letter for the lieutenant relating our voyage thus far.

Now only ten men accompanied me.* We still had five sledges bearing five heavily laden kayaks. Nothing else had changed. The terrain was rarely flat enough for us to take all the sledges with us at once. We still needed to do two trips daily, and occasionally even three. When the wind was in the right quarter, we would hoist sails on the sledges, which made our task easier, if only a little.

The arrival of spring was apparent even at this latitude. It was almost with us. The noontime rays of the sun were warming, but the thaw had not yet begun. The surface of the snow now was covered with a fine crust, smooth and dull, which gave off a dazzling reflection.

At the end of April we all suffered in varying degrees from snow blindness that greatly affected our vision. We had no effective sunglasses. Our mechanic had fabricated some with pieces of green glass scavenged from gin bottles, but they were essentially worthless. As we stumbled our way across the uneven surface of the ice, the danger of snow blindness became very real. Those of us who could still see had to go ahead of the others as scouts. But there

---

* Piotr Maximov, Yan Regald, Prokhor Bayev, Alexander Arhireyev, Olger Nilsen, Pavel Smirennikov, Vladimir Gubanov, Alexander Konrad, Yevgeni Shpakovsky, and Ivan Lunayev.

were days when we were all suffering, and then the only answer was to call a halt and close ourselves up in the tent. The damage to our eyes occurred even when the sky was quite cloudy, and once our vision was affected, everything seemed to be veiled in fog.

————

A scene from this period remains permanently etched upon my memory. Ahead of us, the pack ice stretched into the distance as far as the eye could see. As I could distinguish nothing very clearly, my companion explained to me that there were huge blocks of ice heaped up in layers in the far distance. If we could get to the top of one of those icy towers, I thought, we might be able to spot land, or at least an even higher vantage point. Our five kayaks formed a long ribbon: Mine was being pulled by three sailors, and the others by couples. The weather was fine, warm, and windless, without a single cloud in the sky. The sun was dazzling. I had closed my eyes and pulled my cap well down over my forehead, but the intense light even penetrated my eyelids. From time to time I would open my eyes to check our heading. We strode rhythmically at a good walking pace, hauling strenuously on our ropes, with one hand bracing the kayak atop the sledge. In my right hand I held a ski pole which, as we advanced, repeatedly described the same figure with meticulous precision; swinging forward in a semicircle, then tilting slowly backward to be brought to the front again: the same gesture, over and over. It was as if the ski pole, which made an audible creaking sound upon contact with the snow, was measuring the ground we had already covered: a monotonous tune to accompany the travelers across the icy wilderness. They ended up believing that they could even hear the words to the tune "Far to go, so very far!" until all other thoughts faded away and all that seemed important was the same, mechanical gesture. We were all like sleepwalkers, placing one foot in front of the other, straining our bodies forward against our harnesses....

The sun is a ball of flames. It feels like a torrid southern summer.... I can see a port: People are strolling in the shade of the high harbor walls. Shop doors are open wide. Aromas of tropical fruit fill the air with their fragrance. Peaches, oranges, apricots, raisins, cloves, and pepper all give off their wonderful scents. The asphalt steams after being sprayed with water. I can hear the strident, guttural tones of Persian merchants offering their wares. My God! How marvelous it smells here! How pleasant is the tropical air!

Suddenly my foot tripped over my ski pole. I quickly steadied myself against the kayak, opened my eyes wide, and was dazzled by the sun. For a moment I did not know where I was. What had happened to my tropical port? How the devil had I been transported to this icy wasteland?

"What happened?" asked my companions. "Nothing," I answered, "I tripped over my pole." The boreal landscape unfolded once more before me in an infinite expanse, and the sun which had fleetingly brought me such joy now sought only to blind and torture me.

Yet the hallucination did not completely vanish. My nose was still filled with the aromas of Mediterranean fruit. My companions were not conscious of my present condition. What did it mean? Was I ill? I shut my eyes tight once again. I was like an automaton, moving rhythmically with the pole in my right hand, and once again I could hear the monotonous tune: "Far to go, so very far!"

But what I had just experienced continued to trouble me. For strangely enough I had never liked those aromatic fruits: They had never tempted my palate. But I decided that as soon as I arrived home I would head south and find employment somewhere on the Caspian Sea, where I could gorge on apricots, oranges, and grapes, to make up for the years I had neglected them. Why had I come to this frozen wilderness on the edge of an icy sea, when the weather was so beautiful in the sunny lands to the south? What madness! Tonight we have a "cold evening" ahead of us, since we have no fuel whatsoever. There is not even enough to melt ice for drinking water. But what good would complaining do? All this torture is simply deserved retribution. One should not poke one's nose into places where Nature does not want the presence of man. My one and only goal was to press onward and thereby escape the claws of death. Here I was, dreaming of the sunny south, and I had not yet even left the north! I was now headed for lands far removed from this perilous frozen plain, a place where I might catch the last sweet chords of that tumultuous life I had imagined. How happy I would be simply to feel solid earth beneath my feet once more.

In the meantime we had reached the hummocks of ice we had long been heading for. Now we would have to find a route through them.

It would soon be time to pitch camp, and this seemed like a good, sheltered spot. Our long, exhausting march had brought us less than four miles. We checked to see if we had any superfluous equipment that we might burn to provide us with some heat. That day we had no tea to drink, only hot water, and our supper consisted of a pound of biscuits and a tablespoon of frozen butter each. Soon we slipped into our malitsi to sleep off our fatigue and discouragement. The next morning I awoke feeling quite refreshed. I had had a very optimistic dream. I immediately described it to my companions, who attached a great deal of importance to it. In fact, each of them bound his destiny to the flimsiest of threads!

In my dream I saw all of us crossing endless pack ice with our sledges. In the distance I could see a large crowd of people who were watching something intently and chatting with animation among themselves. They seemed to be waiting for something, so they paid no attention to us, and we did not heed them either. As we drew near, we asked if they were waiting for someone or something. And one of them, pointing to a scrawny old man with white hair who had just appeared from behind a block of ice, replied, "He is a fortune-teller."

Not wishing to let this lucky opportunity slip by, I approached the old man and asked him to tell us our fortune, to tell us whether we would reach land and be saved. At the same time, I held out my hands with the palms up, as one normally does before a soothsayer. The old man glanced briefly at my hands, then pointed to the south with his right hand and said, "You will reach your goal, open water is not far away, but there . . ." and his sentence broke off as I awoke.

My story immediately erased the previous evening's discouragement, and everyone experienced a new burst of courage and enthusiasm for our cause. I, too, was influenced by the optimistic theme of my dream; I was certain that it had been Saint Nicholas himself who had appeared before me to reveal the outcome of our enterprise. Of course, I may have simply been ill at the time, as my hallucinatory state the previous day had shown; but from then on I would never forget that dream. It was still vivid in my memory, despite all our trials and tribulations, when we finally arrived safe and sound at Cape Flora. My traveling companions also gained renewed strength from my dream, and their confidence grew even greater when on that same evening we came upon a large polynya,* where we were able to shoot some seals, which gave us a supply of fresh meat and blubber for fuel. We were happy to be able to eat our fill for once and enjoy a good rest. The disastrous state of the terrain we had to cross often depressed us, but our spirits revived rapidly and we found new energy whenever we met with unexpected good fortune.

———

The expanse of open water before us was extremely vast, and the pack ice on its opposite side was only vaguely discernible on the southern horizon. For several days now the north wind had been blowing, sending smears of grease ice and thickening clumps of frazil ice† streaming across the polynya like a frozen porridge. Through the binoculars one could see that a large quantity of this

---

* A polynya is an area of consistently open water amid the ice pack, prevented from freezing over by prevailing winds and currents.

† Grease ice is a thin film of ice that forms on the surface of the ocean in strips or patches, and indicates the onset of ice formation. Frazil ice is created as grease ice thickens into nascent floes.

"ice porridge," badly shattered, had accumulated on the far side of the polynya; since there was a significant swell running, the heaving movement of the grease ice was clearly visible. We launched one of the kayaks and tried to paddle across the polynya, but quickly became convinced that it would be impossible to penetrate the ice porridge, which extended for half a mile from the southern side of the open water. Thus we had to search for a route around the polynya. To the east, the open water extended for many miles. We walked for six nautical miles without seeing its far shore, the water being hidden under a heavy layer of frost smoke. Patches of water sky were visible above the eastern horizon. To the west, the expanse of water grew narrower, but still seemed endless after three miles of walking. There were large numbers of beluga and minke whales in the polynya. Every minute one would hear them blowing. They would rush back and forth in pods, breaching the ocean's surface, then disappear into the depths again.

We also saw many seals, but always at a distance. If one starts whistling at them, however, as if to a horse one is leading to water, the seals will approach, evidently intrigued, peering curiously with heads held high. In this fashion we were able to kill four or five of them. To our delight, this lucky catch greatly enriched our dwindling reserves of flesh and blubber, and we could look forward to several days of abundant and nourishing food.

Whether boiled or roasted, seal meat remains dark and tender, with a pleasant taste, similar to venison, at least as far as the animals we killed to the north of Franz Josef Land were concerned; seal meat I had eaten in the Kara Sea often had an oily, blubbery taste, even after being left a long time to marinate in vinegar. Polar bear meat is without a doubt much tastier, although it also takes on an oily taste if it is kept for any time after it has been cooked, especially the meat near the bone. This difference in taste probably depends on the environment in which the animal is found, as well as its diet. In the stomachs of all the seals we killed north of Franz Josef Land—and that was a considerable number—we invariably found the remains of small crustaceans, but never any fish. In my opinion, seal meat is entirely edible; the liver of the seal is even a delicacy. All of us on the ship ate it with relish, even when we still had abundant and varied provisions. Seal brains fried in seal oil also taste very good. The front flippers, well baked, are reminiscent of calves' feet.

Initially my companions overindulged in seal blubber. They would cut it into small pieces and fry it thoroughly, producing what is called cracklings. If they ate them with ship's biscuits, they would quickly become sated. But we were rationing biscuits, so the cracklings were often eaten alone, just with salt. This delicacy has a pronounced effect on a stomach that is unaccustomed to it, like a powerful laxative. Eventually, however, one's stomach gets used to anything, and we found we could eat the cracklings with impunity.

During the full two days we camped beside this stretch of open water, the grease ice and frazil ice congealed into a thin but solid surface that spanned the polynya's narrower, western reaches, allowing us to finally haul our sledges across it. Once on the far side, we pressed onward in a slightly more easterly direction, hoping to find a greater expanse of open water, but this goal eluded us. Now and then we would encounter small polynyas in which we could shoot seals for food and fuel, but none permitted us to travel far in our kayaks.

Death of Sailor Bayev, Further Discouragement, Exhaustion

Here we were, once again making our way across the pack from ice floe to ice floe, sinking into deep snow. Our sledges, made with improvised tools, were simply not up to the task; every day we had to stop for long and complicated repairs. Fortunately we had reinforced the runners with iron strips; when the runners broke, the only way we could repair them was to screw the metal strips back onto the shattered runners, thereby holding the damaged sections together, however tenuously.

But the month of May had arrived. It was at around this time that the sailor Bayev asked me to head in a more westerly direction because, according to his observations, there were long uninterrupted stretches of ice to be found in that direction which would speed up our progress. "They are," he insisted, "as flat as a skating rink." I gave in to his request, but although we headed westward for an entire day, the promised stretches of smooth ice did not appear. Bayev insisted that his level ice field really existed. "I saw it with my own eyes, sir. I skied along it myself. It stretched all the way to the island."

The next day, May 3, I resolved to head more to the south-southeast, to search for a better route. Bayev again asked permission to explore the terrain to the west.

With several companions, I set out to the south-southeast. We found a fairly practicable route, and returned to our bivouac after three hours. Bayev was not there. Noon came, and still he had not arrived. At four P.M., sure that something was amiss, we decided to search for the missing man.

Taking some biscuits, Regald, Konrad, Shpakovsky, and I set off on the trail. Bayev was not a good skier, and he had left his skis behind. We could easily follow the tracks of his skin boots in the deep snow. At first they led to the south-west, but gradually curved to the west. About three miles from camp we encountered thin ice with very little snow on it. Bayev had followed the left edge of these ice fields, apparently in the hope that they would swing toward the south, but ice blocks continued to obstruct his route.

In the meantime the weather had deteriorated, and snow had begun to fall. We soon ran across small leads, which we crossed on skis with no problem; but Bayev would have had to cross them by hopping from floe to floe. We followed Bayev's trail for two hours, having covered at least six to eight miles. Finally the tracks turned back, but Bayev had not retraced his outbound route, veering instead to the left. Our flag, hoisted atop an ice hummock near camp, had long since disappeared from view behind the pressure ridges. Now Bayev's track grew faint, as fresh snow covered it: We would find a few footprints, then lose the track altogether. The snow had even begun to obliterate our own tracks. We shouted, whistled, and fired our guns without success. Bayev had a rifle with about twelve shells with him. Had he been nearby, he would have heard our shots and responded in kind. But we heard nothing.

We hurried back to the camp to resort to other methods of rescue. There, with the help of long sticks and ski poles, I raised a mast thirty feet high with two signal flags that could be seen from a great distance. If Bayev was lost not far from the camp, he could not fail to see them and would easily find his way back to us. Moreover, the weather was improving by the hour. When Bayev had not returned by late evening, we became increasingly worried. The night did not calm our anxiety. At first light we once more began to explore the area around us, but without success. We waited three days, still hoping to see him reappear. We could only assume that he must have fallen through a fissure in the ice. Perhaps he succumbed to the shock of the icy water, for he had often complained of a bad heart.

We had done everything in our power to save him. Now all that I could do was to organize our departure, in order not to further endanger the lives of those who remained. This sad turn of events was enough in itself to dampen the men's spirits; they sincerely regretted the loss of their companion, who had set off with such noble intentions, only to meet his death.

To continue my story, I refer to the notes in my diary:

MAY 14

We are continuing our journey, but have traveled only two and a half miles in six hours. Today is a noteworthy day because we are now sixty nautical miles* away from the *Saint Anna,* but we have mixed feelings as we realize that despite all our efforts, our average progress has been only two miles a day! Nevertheless we celebrated the event with a soup made from dried cherries and blueberries, enhanced with a bit of condensed milk, and a rye biscuit. The wind is blowing from the northwest, and the temperature is dropping. To the south we can see a vast water sky.

MAY 15

We will once again have to make do with a cold meal due to lack of fuel. This precarious situation is extremely upsetting to me, since I am entirely responsible for it. I find it odd that this fails to worry my companions. Not only are they incapable of any serious thoughts, but they also lack determination and enterprising spirit. Their interest in our daily tasks is solely motivated by their desire to reach home: Serious or critical situations drain them of all their strength. My concern for their future is sometimes an enormous burden to me, but they scarcely realize it!

Today we have covered just over a mile; cold, misty weather.

MAY 16

Further calamitous events! Yesterday three of the men almost drowned. Fortunately, their shipmates were able to rescue them in time. But our shotgun and "stove" were immersed in corrosive seawater, and most of our remain-

---

* The significance of this to Albanov was that sixty nautical miles equals one degree of latitude.

ing fuel was lost. As a result, our meat must now be eaten raw. We have reached the end of the polynya, and must continue our trek without further delay. The entire region is shrouded in fog; not long ago we could still see a lot of water sky.

MAY 17

Yesterday our kayaks hardly made any headway as the water was obstructed by chunks of ice, which made our crossing particularly difficult. Today we were luckier and were able to paddle roughly six miles to the south-southwest. Our kayaks have been very useful; we can fit all our belongings in the bottom of their hulls and then sit comfortably on top of them. Although our craft are not completely waterproof, they transport us quickly and safely wherever we find a favorable lead.

I paddled ahead of the others with the sailor Nilsen. When we reached the edge of the open water, I climbed on top of a high block of ice to search the horizon. I could see only two of our kayaks, the other two being probably too far away. Two hours went by, and the kayaks still had not arrived.

What had happened? Finally two kayaks approached the shore, and we learned the cause of the delay. Alone in his boat, our steward Regald had not been able to resist the temptation of clambering up onto an iceberg. When he was ready to get back into his kayak, the edge of the block of ice split and Regald took an involuntary plunge into the cold water. He managed to heave himself back onto the ice, but as the wind had driven his boat away, the other kayak had to save him and recapture his drifting boat. Soaked to the skin, Regald was in great danger of freezing to death, so we pitched the tent and lit a fire as quickly as possible, which also allowed us to cook a dish of peas on a makeshift stove.

This unplanned halt was a great irritation to me. My companions are no better than children: As if it were not enough to endure our numerous involuntary setbacks—they seem to cause still others just for the sake of it. I certainly will not rest until I've managed to save them in spite of themselves.

Toward evening, a wind from the southeast picked up, bringing a light snowfall.

SUNDAY, MAY 18

Today we reached some excellent terrain and were able to continue without interruption across a fine layer of fresh ice as smooth as a mirror, which supported us nicely, as it was unfractured and about six inches thick. This reminded me of the fact that Nansen, in Hvidtenland,* had also encountered similar ice conditions. It was surely not the same kind of ice here as that which had trapped the *Saint Anna.* Hauling three of our sledges over this solid layer, we were able to travel on a straight course for four hours, and covered roughly four and a quarter miles before reaching a new open lead, where we called a halt. I decided to stay there with Lunayev to shoot some game while the other eight went back for the two remaining sledges. How often had I pondered in vain on a way to re-

---

* An island group in northeast Franz Josef Land, the first land that Nansen came to on his journey south (see map).

solve this useless waste of time and energy! We just could
not go on like this. Besides, Lunayev was so weak that he
could hardly stand. Without further hesitation, I sacrificed a sledge and a kayak for fuel so that there would be
only four sledges and four kayaks for the ten of us, and
that would have to suffice, come what may.

MAY 19

We have not made a move all day. We lashed all our belongings onto the four sledges and inspected the lead to
see if we should go around or across it. I fell through the
ice twice during our investigations. Soundings were
taken, but our line measured only 110 fathoms and could
not reach the bottom. There were pools of open water in
every direction, and the gloomy weather greatly reduced
visibility. For nineteen days I have been unable to take a
proper sun sight, or calculate our position, or—most important of all—ascertain our progress toward the south.

We calculated today that we have 460 pounds of biscuits left, which should be sufficient for one month. If we
manage to shoot some more seals or polar bears, we will
be able to reduce our daily ration of biscuit. It is strange
that, despite encountering so much open water, we have
found no seals; as for bears, we have seen only their tracks,
which means they must be hiding in their lairs. White
gulls and fulmars often fly overhead in pairs or even three
at a time; diving birds such as auks, however, have suddenly disappeared. All these impressions do nothing to
improve my faith in the outcome of our ordeal. In these
inhospitable latitudes, one must be prepared for daily
surprises that can destroy the best-laid plans. Moreover,

winds from the north and northeast can drive us appreciably and unpredictably toward the south and southwest. We have just come upon a channel, which if it continues toward the south, will allow us to make better progress and offers the possibility of shooting a bear.

Each of our sledges now has a load of about 240 pounds, a weight that two men can haul under any circumstances. We are all tormented by terrible pain in our eyes, and Lunayev still has severe leg pains. Are we going to have to carry him on a sledge? Our scouts have just returned with the news that it is possible to go around the open lead that blocks our path. Southeasterly wind blowing, force 4,* working against us.

MAY 20

No change in the wind. Dull weather, sky somewhat overcast. We set off with all the sledges at once, but the route quickly became so bad that we again had to resort to taking them in stages. Toward evening, our difficulties increased still further, and we struggled to make the slightest headway. There was a huge polynya ahead of us, from which we were separated by many small leads and crevasses. We had come to realize that the various ice floes were all subject to constant movement, and that new floes were continually forming.

We pitched our tent to have a rest. Shpakovsky and I went out to search for a safe route for the next day, and we managed to find one.

---

* Force 4 on the Beaufort scale is a "moderate breeze" of 11 to 16 knots (13 to 18 mph).

Lunayev's condition is more and more worrying: He complains of pains in his legs, and is suffering from snow blindness. I am afraid we may soon have to strap him to a sledge. Our greatest hope lies in finding the landmass we have been seeking for so long, where we shall be saved from our fears of drifting ever northward.

MAY 21

We managed to bypass the dangerous waters, but at the expenditure of a great deal of sweat! Six or seven of us at a time had to strain hard to get each sledge over myriad ice ridges, crevasses, and holes. The entire way we had to carve a passable route from the pack ice, chipping away with our axes and harpoons. It was a far cry from the smooth, snow-free terrain where we needed only two men to pull each sledge. We were blocked at every stride by unforeseen channels and fissures, and today we covered only four miles. The horizon reveals a water sky. Ahead of us lie numerous open leads too wide to be bridged by a sledge, yet too narrow and choked with ice blocks to be navigable by kayak. The appearance of our surroundings has changed dramatically. No sign of thick pack ice. Everywhere there is fresh, bluish sheet ice between one and nine inches thick. Today it is even mixed with sand and clay.*

When I was with Lunayev today I noticed he was spitting blood. I examined him at once and found that his gums bore the characteristic symptoms of scurvy.

At least I now have a clear idea of what is wrong with him, and there is only one remedy: a lot of physical move-

---

* Sand and clay in the ice would signal the presence of nearby land.

ment! But I also managed to make him take some quinine. His recovery depends on the strength of his physical resistance and his will to live.

My instruments are in a sorry state. The big compass was broken and quite useless so I threw it out. The small one is hardly any better: The glass is broken and the liquid has seeped out. The magnet stone at the tip of the needle has been damaged by the repeated battering it has received, so now the needle scarcely moves at all. To navigate I have been forced to rely on little more than the sun, my watch, and the miniature compass fitted onto my binoculars. But these minor setbacks would be bearable if we had confidence that we were getting nearer to our destination and could see land. Open, Sesame!

Toward evening, the wind backed to the northeast. Thank God!

MAY 22

The wind has shifted again, and is now blowing from the east-northeast, which is quite bad news since it can force us to drift westward. It has gotten much colder. The terrain, on the whole, is good. Only rarely do we have to cross thin, brittle ice; the underlayer sometimes has a brownish color, which we mistakenly thought was sand or clay. On closer examination we realized it was a pinkish brown algae, which led us to the conclusion that the ice had been near a coastline. Later, this coloring would become more frequent.

The fog finally lifted and the sun came out, but I was unable to calculate the meridian altitude; I could do no more than reckon that we were at latitude 82°38′ north.

At midnight I obtained the sun's altitude and got a latitude of 82°29′, a coordinate which seemed more exact. Without an artificial horizon, and with an overcast sky, I had to be content with these approximate observations. That is not all that is missing. Above all, we lack good sledges... and good sledge dogs.

The wind backed again to the northeast and filled our sails. What an interesting picture our little fleet made as it raised its sails! But I can hardly say, as Nansen did, "In the gusts we often went along like feathers." It was really more like crawling, but the sails did help us a little to haul our loads, and on the whole they did make things easier. We followed our route all day long, and did not see any sign of seals. We observed only an unknown species of seagull.

Gubanov has now also contracted scurvy, his gums bleeding and swollen, so I have decided to use the two invalids as scouts, to keep them on the move. I realized that there had already been cases of scurvy back on board the *Saint Anna*, and it was the lieutenant no doubt who had been the most seriously afflicted. Brusilov had been ill for six or seven months. For three months straight, he had lain flat on his back, unable to muster the strength to turn over. To accomplish this, one man had to stand on the bed straddling his legs and lift him by the hips, while another turned him by the shoulders. We had to put soft pillows under all his limbs, since he had begun to develop bedsores.

Any sudden movement caused Brusilov pain: He would curse and shout terribly. To bathe him, we had to lower him into the bathtub on a sheet. To picture him in February 1913, imagine a skeleton covered not with skin but with rubber, from which every joint and bone protruded. When the sun rose we tried to open the portholes in his cabin, but he took a strange aversion to daylight and demanded that the portholes be shut tight and the lamp lit. Nothing could arouse him from sleep during the day; he showed no interest in anything. He refused all food: One had to persuade him, like a small child, to try an egg or some bouillon, and threaten him with no dessert.

He would spend the day sleeping and the night in a delirious trance. In this delirium, he would at first talk quite rationally and seem to be in a good mood. Then suddenly he would begin to ask how many whales and walruses we had killed during the third winter at the mouth of the Yenesei, how many sturgeon we had caught there and sold. Or he would ask me whether the horses had been given hay or oats. "But what horses are you talking about, Georgiy L'vovich? We don't possess a single horse. We're in the Kara Sea aboard *Saint Anna*." "Oh, don't give me that story," he would respond.

It was mainly our nurse, Miss Zhdanko, who tirelessly nursed the invalid, and who had to suffer his outbursts of anger. She had a hard time of it. When healthy, Brusilov was refined, courteous, and tactful, but when ill, he became extremely coarse. He would hurl cups and plates at the nurse, if she cajoled him to drink some soup. But she bore it all with patience.

But I will return to my diary.

Those who suffer from scurvy not only need to keep moving, but also need good food, and this was a great worry to me, as our meat powder was running out, and our supplies of condensed milk and chocolate were also dwindling. And it was precisely this dried food source that would have been the best adapted for our meals, which the travails and hectic pace of our journey did not always allow us much time to prepare.

MAY 23

In the morning, the weather was fine and clear. Our scouts promised us smooth travel, and they were right, for we covered five whole miles between ten in the morning and six-thirty in the evening. The northeast wind continued to blow steadily, which was a great blessing, since it forced the ice floes tight together, thereby reducing the width of crevasses and open leads, allowing our sledges to run smoothly. Toward noon I took a sun sight and found a latitude of 82°31′ north. To the south, the horizon was crystal clear with no water sky. I had the impression that the ice had stopped drifting southward with the wind, probably because it had encountered some resistance—which in my opinion could only come from a landmass. But this opinion remained mere speculation, since all the goodwill in the world had not permitted me to find land up to now! There were no signs of life whatsoever. We had spotted a few bear tracks, but not a single seal.

Our supplies were diminishing at an alarming rate. All that remained were six pounds of meat powder, three tins of condensed milk, and roughly two pounds of dried apples. The last of the chocolate was handed out today. All we have left for our main source of nourishment are ship's biscuits.

I hear constant conversations about the tastiest foods the men can imagine. Involuntarily, I start to think of such treats myself. Life on land, with all its comforts and charms, seems so magnificent and enticing that I begin to doubt whether we shall ever reach that happy place.

Why are all these delights of life on land so clear before my eyes right now, like hallucinations? Is this the end already? Is this a premonition of our deaths? No, it cannot be! I am convinced that we will reach land sooner or later. On the march I have become religious as never before, almost superstitious. My icon of Nicholas the Miracle-worker is always in my pocket. But my men grow abject and despondent, no matter how I try to cheer them up.

A northerly wind began to blow toward evening. The ice seems to be on the move again: We have blundered off route into very unpleasant terrain. Soft snow and a great many pools of water did not make our task any easier. Nilsen and I have been trying to level the track out for those following us. It was hard work, and we are exhausted. I need to change our methods: Henceforth three men will pull the first sledge and the others will follow immediately behind. They will move faster in the tracks of those ahead, and will not have to pull so hard.

Drifting Southward

The first of June is my saint's day. What a wonderful gift of Providence it would be if we could reach the 82nd parallel by that day!

MAY 24

During a dead calm, a thick fog rolled in during the night. Earlier I had noticed vast patches of water sky, while a remarkably luminous cloud floated above the horizon to the south and south-southeast. The cloud was concave in the middle and its edges blended into the horizon but it stood out very clearly. I observed it attentively through the binoculars but finally gave up all hopes of discerning land. And yet this unusual cloud might have been the reflection of a glacier lying on solid earth!

Yesterday evening I decided to increase our speed, but I must concede already that the best intentions do not automatically bring the desired results. The conditions have deteriorated so dramatically that it now requires a superhuman effort to force the sledges through the snow, which has become extremely slushy underneath. If that were not bad enough, wretched polynyas constantly hinder our sluggish progress, forcing us to make huge detours that do nothing to keep us from sinking into the slush. The kayaks are useless for crossing the polynyas, moreover, because of dangerous chunks of floating ice. Despite untold efforts we have advanced little more than two and a half miles to the south. We halted at the edge of a particularly bad stretch of open water and set up camp.

Fog all day long, with that dull light that makes one's eyes so terribly painful. At the moment mine hurt so much that I see this diary only as through a veil, and hot tears run down my cheeks. From time to time I have to stop writing and bury my head in my malitsa. Only in complete darkness does the pain gradually abate, allowing me to open my eyes again.

In the morning the wind was out of the northwest, but veered to the northeast in the afternoon, and the horizon was quite dark. We tried to gauge the depth of the water, but our sounding line was too short. This abortive effort nevertheless allowed us to conclude that we were drifting noticeably southward, for the plumb line was definitely tilted toward the north. We also tried to shoot a few auks and a seal; but Diana must not have been pleased with us, for our prey escaped and we were left empty-handed.

Tomorrow the civilized world will be celebrating Pentecost. How delightful it must be in the south, while we languish here so miserably, drifting at latitude 82°30' north.

SUNDAY, MAY 25

Whitsunday: Today we were overjoyed. First of all we came upon the sort of lead that is normally difficult to cross, and yet we managed to dispatch it with relative ease and advance nearly two miles toward the south. One of the men came with me in my kayak. As soon as we had crossed the channel I disembarked, took a noon sight, and found 82°21′. I could not believe my eyes and immediately suspected an error. But a second calculation confirmed the first result. I had not been mistaken. This was a great surprise, a real Whitsuntide treat. And that would not be the only one, for soon the men in the last kayak came to tell me that they had shot a polar bear!

This announcement was indeed very welcome news to us all. The last time we had eaten roasted bear had been on board the *Saint Anna*, around September last year, and today we would again be very gratefully sitting down to a wonderfully plentiful meal—what inexpressible joy! Just as we had been picturing the future with grave concern, good fortune had sent us this "royal dish," as Sverdrup* called it, which, in addition to feeding us, would provide us with fuel. Three kayaks immediately made ready to go back for the precious bounty, whose hide and fat would help us keep warm. We cut up the rest according to the rules of the meat-cutter's art. The most skilled master butcher could not have done better. We removed the

* The Norwegian Otto Sverdrup was one of the greatest Arctic explorers. He had skied across Greenland with Nansen in 1888, and had been captain on board the *Fram* when Nansen and Johansen made their bold attempt on the North Pole in 1895 (see Introduction). During 1914–15 he led an unsuccessful search for Brusilov and Albanov's lost party.

magnificent pelt, along with fat, to use as fuel (the skin, worth 200 rubles, had to be burned to save our own skins). The blood was collected in containers, and that same evening we had a choice of boiled or roasted bear meat. The liver, eaten raw with salt, is a real delicacy! The men were completely transformed. A boisterous good humor replaced their disheartened lassitude; hope and courage blossomed before my eyes. Their spirits soared. I would never have believed that they could have enjoyed themselves so much. Heaven had sent us succor at a time of utter distress, and our gratitude for this miraculous gift was apparent in our overflowing happiness.

The wind seems to be shifting; sometimes it blows from the south, sometimes the southwest or east-southeast. The sky is clear, the sun even feels hot, and the entire landscape sparkles with a dazzling whiteness, which is unbearably painful to our unprotected eyes.

MAY 26

We are still at the same camp, cutting up the bear meat. There is a flurry of activity both outside and inside the tent. Cooking, roasting, melting the fat, etc. I have been trying to dry some strips of meat in the wind. Now that we have at last been able to eat our fill, our energy and confidence in the face of danger have once more gained the upper hand.

Four of our men went looking for a good route. The weather is still excellent today, very clear with a strong northerly wind. Although my eyes are very sore, I was able, with great difficulty, to take a sun sight that gave me a reading of latitude 82°20′ north. The wind has therefore pushed us southward one whole nautical mile over the last twenty-four hours. As I walked with my sextant to a nearby observation site, I noticed the tracks of two polar bears.

MAY 27

Yesterday we struck camp at ten P.M. to continue our route toward the south. But we were forced to stop after three hours because there was so much shattered ice that we could not continue. Wind again from the west.

I will have to take back my praise for polar bear liver! On board the *Saint Anna* there had been rumors about the drawbacks or even the dangers of eating it. We had paid little heed to them then, and in any case at that time had no opportunity to taste it. Now I am convinced that the warnings were well founded. Bear liver is obviously very harmful to one's health. All those who ate it came down with headaches and dizzy spells, as if we had been poisoned by carbon monoxide. The discomfort spread throughout the body and our stomachs suffered dreadfully. We were forced to accept the truth of the proverb that wisdom comes only through hardship, and I swore never again to eat bear liver, no matter how much it might tempt my palate.*

Another violent snowstorm during the night.

---

* Albanov had good reason to be wary of polar bear liver, which we now know can carry a lethal overdose of vitamin A. In 1897, the Swede Salomon Andrée and two companions, attempting to balloon to the North Pole, vanished northwest of Franz Josef Land. Thirty-three years later, their last camp on White Island was discovered by accident, the men's skeletons intact. So well preserved were the trio's belongings that film in their camera was successfully developed. The cause of the men's deaths seemed puzzling, for they were found with ample food and supplies. A photo from the camera, showing two men standing over a dead polar bear, was corroborated by Andrée's diary entry bragging of the kill, only six days before some fatal catastrophe struck the party. These clues lend credence to the hypothesis that a vitamin A overdose caused their deaths.

MAY 28

The blizzard continued into the day and kept us in our tent until noon. The wind shifted first to the south then the east. In the afternoon we risked a departure and were plagued for the rest of the day by innumerable cracks and channels. It was hard work. Often our feet would plunge into a foot of water beneath the slushy snow. In spite of all our efforts we got no farther than two and a half miles; we were exhausted and soaked to the skin. We tried taking a depth sounding, but the plumb line was still not on the bottom at seventy fathoms, though the line's angle through the water confirmed that we were drifting southward once again.

Despite this heartening conclusion, our situation was hardly to be envied. Nobody had any doubts about that, and I was not at all surprised when the sailor Konrad, followed by four other crewmen, came to see me that evening to express their wish to abandon the kayaks and sledges and continue on skis. Although I thought it extremely risky to resort to such measures at this stage, I could not refuse their request, given the fact that my way of doing things held equally scant promise of success.

I put forward a few objections, explaining that—depending on the circumstances—without kayaks we risked finding ourselves in some very critical situations. I argued that we could still continue pulling the sledges and kayaks, as they were not really that heavy. "Imagine how it will be," I told them, "if we reach land and find ourselves with no warm clothes, no dishes or utensils, no ax, and none of the other important items we now have stowed in the boats." I did not feel that I had convinced the men, but at least they remained silent. We had already started burning parts of our tent, and it would not be long before we dispensed with it. When traveling by kayak, the tent creates a problem because is it very cumbersome and has to be laid in a certain complicated way across the craft, and it is also quite dangerous due to its considerable weight, especially when wet.

An inventory of our supplies has shown that we still have sixteen bags of biscuits, our staple diet, which weigh three hundred and twenty pounds. To that we can add a few bags of ground peas and some bear meat. Our ammunition is almost as heavy as the biscuits. But with the best will in the world we simply cannot eliminate any of these vital items.

MAY 29

Endless channels, cracks, and polynyas have been hampering our progress. The ice pack is breaking up. Nansen told how he found a lot of fractured ice as he approached Franz Josef Land. All the channels lie east-west, not one of them running in the direction we wish to travel. Confronted by this confusion of fragmented ice floes, we feel as if we had been shipwrecked, and we wonder how we will ever find our way to safety.

Lunayev shot two seals today, so we shall now have fresh meat and blubber again for some time. Seal blubber when heated gives a much better light than bear fat; it ignites more easily, gives a clearer flame, and its ashes replace the wick.

The wind is out of the northeast. The ice pack is drifting to the southwest; every day it becomes clearer that we are moving ever southward. My sun sight today gave a position of 82°08.5′. May this good fortune never abandon or deceive us!

MAY 30

At dawn, a northwesterly wind, force 5.* Shortly after breakfast a violent blizzard arose. Nevertheless we prepared our kayaks and set off toward the south, over very difficult terrain. The ice floes are becoming smaller and smaller, forcing us to use our kayaks most of the day. As soon as we cross one stretch of open water, another one immediately becomes visible. Sometimes they are no farther apart than one to two hundred yards. It may be sea ice of this sort, which we are now encountering regularly, that Nansen compared to a fisherman's net. In any case it seems that we are well and truly captured in such a net. May God give us the strength to emerge safe and sound from this unrelenting danger!

Even after pushing ourselves to the limit, today we hauled the sledges no more than two miles, though we are drifting irresistibly southward all the while. Not so long ago I hardly dared entertain the thought that we might reach the 82nd parallel by June 1! What colossal efforts would have been required for us to reach the goal of our dreams solely under our own power! If I compare our daily progress to that of a tortoise, it would be an insult to the poor tortoise. But I was to learn that miracles do exist, for today my noon calculation situated us at

---

* Force 5 on the Beaufort scale is a "fresh breeze" of 17 to 21 knots (20 to 24 mph).

82°01′, and as I write these lines, we have certainly drifted south of 82°!

If I look at my map, the extreme northern point of Prince Rudolf Land is situated at 82°12′. As we have already passed below 82°, that land must either be to the east or to the west of us; probably to the east, if our calculations of the *Saint Anna*'s drift were accurate. I am certain that we are drifting westward, as proved by the prevailing winds, the constant inclination of my sounding line, and even my chronometer, which has now become all but useless. My map shows two peaks of over twelve hundred feet on Prince Rudolf Land. If my figures are correct, I should have been able to see those peaks long ago, and yet I have seen nothing of the sort.

But my navigational tools are now almost worthless. What would I not give for a good chart and an accurate chronometer! Still, even if I had had a better timepiece, it probably would not have withstood the constant battering. The only service this particular chronometer has rendered is to prove, each time I shoot the sun, that we are almost always drifting to the west. Inside my kayak, it has also functioned as a most comfortable seat!

If we do manage to reach land and determine our coordinates, I should be able to trace our course on the map without error. Scanning the horizon for some sign of land is thus extremely important. But I cannot expect much assistance from my comrades in this regard, for they remain curiously indifferent to such matters. Hoping to persuade them to search the horizon from the top of a high block of ice now and then, I have promised twenty-five rubles to the first man who sights land.

We spent the night at the very edge of a narrow lead. The wind was blowing from the northwest, force 6.* We saw polar bear tracks in three different places.

MAY 31

We had just finished our breakfast when Maximov rushed into the tent shouting that he had spotted a huge bear on the opposite side of the lead. Lunayev and I jumped up, grabbed our rifles, and ran out, hiding behind blocks of ice. We waited in silence, but when we spotted the animal, it was out of range. We were in a favorable position, however, which allowed us to follow the bear's every movement. He raised his muzzle and sniffed the wind. The smell of roasted fat coming from our camp clearly enticed him, but he could not decide whether to move closer. If it had not been for three black spots on his head and the yellowish tinge of his fur, he would have blended in perfectly with his icy backdrop. Only his nose and eyes betrayed his presence as he moved about.

He soon detected our presence and watched us with a lively interest for roughly five minutes. Then suddenly he turned tail and bolted for safety. There was no time to lose; we had to attack. We both fired simultaneously and hit our target. The gigantic animal fell, but got up again right away and began to trot off. So we fired off a few more rounds in succession: The bear fell once more and rolled head over heels, but again got up to flee the danger zone. He was so badly wounded, however, that this new attempt at flight was unsuccessful; he could no longer

---

* Force 6 on the Beaufort scale is a "strong breeze" of 22 to 27 knots (25 to 31 mph).

stand, and after writhing about and biting the ice, he soon lay motionless. We immediately got into a kayak and rowed to the spot where, by all appearances, he lay dead. But as we drew near, the bear jumped up on his hind legs and ran off as quickly as a racehorse. As we could not pursue him, we returned to the camp, greatly annoyed at this useless waste of ammunition.

After a few minutes, Konrad asked permission to continue the hunt. I agreed but, for his own safety, sent his friend Smirennikov along with him. They quickly found the injured bear, which again tried to run away as they approached, but his strength failed him and after a few steps he fell dead into a pool. We all went together to fetch our magnificent prey, and carefully cut up the carcass back at the camp. Before long the cauldrons were bubbling all around us. Once again we had a superb meal, if quite unexpected, and we ate to our heart's content. But this time, we left the liver for the goddess of the hunt!

Today, May 31, seems to be a very lucky day. In addition to the roast bear that Diana has bestowed upon us, we have enjoyed the distinguished favors of Aeolus, blowing from the north. My calculations showed our latitude to be 81°54′, and it seemed to me, although I could not be certain, that our plumb line touched the sea bed at one hundred fathoms. I harbored the increasingly firm conviction that land must be nearby. All around us Nature had suddenly taken on a new aspect. Various signs of life were replacing the lethal silence that had reigned so far. We often saw birds now, and encountered a good number of seals. Flocks of fulmars flew overhead. These were clear signs that we were approaching those latitudes where the realm of white death would end. The ice was in constant motion, and chunks continually broke away from the large ice floes.

In our camp, too, there were more signs of life today. Cooking utensils played a major role and the steward was displaying his talents. Under his supervision everyone was cooking, roasting, making sausages, or drying meat. The bear we killed today was no less than ten feet long from the tip of the nose to the tail. His pelt is truly beautiful. One would get a lot of money for it in a market. It is a pity that we must abandon it; but it would be impossible to haul such a load with us, now that we are preparing to discard even some of our essentials.

Sadness has given way to exuberant high spirits, and there seems to be a contest to see who could offer the best proof that life is worth living, even in these desolate, far-off regions.

A strong wind out of the north brought a violent snowstorm during the night.

SUNDAY, JUNE 1

My saint's day! Early in the morning everyone began to offer me his best wishes. Our steward, Regald, made an effort to mark the event with a well-prepared banquet. Each of us had an enormous bear steak seasoned with onions, and a hot, juicy sausage, and for dessert we had tea with the last of the dried apples. All the guests were in a very festive mood, which was bolstered by a favorable wind driving us relentlessly southward. It was almost as though all we had to do was to sit in our tent and wait, as if a postal coach were delivering us slowly but surely to our destination. Latitude 81°49.5′.

We are indeed drifting continually southward. But I have been worried by a secondary phenomenon that, for the moment, I have kept hidden from my companions. The ice is drifting to the south-southwest and clearly there are no obstacles to stop its progression. But how are we to reach the archipelago we are so impatiently waiting for! This thought brings bitter pangs of concern. How happy would I have been if our present drift had come to our aid when we were still to the north of Franz Josef Land. Now this rapid southward drift will inevitably cause us to miss land altogether and sweep us into the Barents Sea. In fact, we should have been moving along the western coast of the archipelago, between Franz Josef Land and Svalbard. Surprisingly, during the last few days, the ice has been moving in a very irregular fashion, which may be due to the tides.

The possibility still remains that the ice may come into contact with the shore, no doubt very far away. All these unanswered questions depress me greatly at times. Anyone who has been in a position to observe the immensity of Nature's power feels intimidated by his own perceptions—as if giants were testing their strength by playing with each other on a colossal chessboard. I will try to give an example: In exploring the region to the south-southeast, we were surprised to discover ski tracks on one of the ice floes. Closer examination convinced us that we were looking at our own tracks, and that this ice floe had caught up with us as a result of a change of current. How is one supposed to proceed over this sort of ice? On the surface, one achieves no more success than a squirrel in a wheel-cage. Even our reconnaissance forays are dangerous: If one goes too far from camp, one can easily get lost.

Today we took a sounding but did not reach the bottom with a 100-fathom line. On our scouting trip we saw the fresh tracks of a female bear with two cubs, as well as the tracks of three other adult bears. Lunayev shot a seal, but before it could be retrieved, it sank. The north wind blew constantly throughout the evening, and snow fell during the night.

JUNE 2

At dawn the north wind turns into a howling gale. Screeching and wailing, it heaps up sheets of ice like playing cards, and shakes our tent with blustering violence, making it crack and strain. There is water rushing everywhere. It would be pointless to attempt to take out the kayaks. The ice driven by the storm does not seem to be encountering any obstacles to the south-southwest. The open sea must lie in that direction.

I took advantage of a few moments of relative calm to make some celestial observations and came up with 81°42.5′. We have moved seven nautical miles to the south in the last twenty-four hours. Where can we be? Surely to the west of the Franz Josef archipelago. Perhaps we are somewhere to the north of Alexandra Land. We can only hope that we are not too far west, somewhere between Franz Josef Land and Svalbard. Then we would be in a bad mess—we might miss Franz Josef Land altogether and still not reach Svalbard.

If I am not mistaken, Nansen saw land when traveling with Johansen from his winter quarters on Jackson Island toward Cape Flora. It must have been low-lying land, covered in ice and snow. It would be wonderful if we could find Nansen's route, for then I could refer to his observations, which I had carefully noted in the diary. I know nothing of Alexandra Land; on my pitiful map, the coast is indicated only by a dotted line. Obviously, it is useless to nurture any suppositions when they cannot be supported by solid proof. We must be patient. Let us wait and see. One thing is certain: We must move southeast, and under no circumstances may we deviate to the west.

It was with mixed feelings that I curled up into my malitsa again today. For the time being we must remain idle, wait for better weather and a better route, and consider ourselves lucky to have been well fed, with enough left over to provide considerable reserves of dried meat. Despite the impossible terrain, Lunayev went out and shot a seal that we will use only for fuel. There were high waves in the lead, and when it came time to retrieve the seal, my "seamen" lost their nerve and hid behind one another. I paddled out alone to encourage them.

For the time being the storm is shrieking its triumphant overture, crushing everything in its path. Thank God we are under cover!

JUNE 4

A strong northerly wind continues to blow, with snow flurries but warmer temperatures. The air is damp both outside and inside the tent, and the ground sheet is soaked, since there is no air blowing through. We have been forced to move the tent to drier positions lately, but that would be useless today, since outside everything is soggy as well. Even our clothes are soaking wet. So we sit together in silence; we feel as if we are clad in damp bandages all day. The weather is just as unbearable inside as out. Even if we had more heat it would not reduce the humidity in the tent, however zealously Lunayev provides us with seal blubber for heating—something which is not all that easy, for the seals are to be found only in the channels, and only very briefly lift their heads out of the water. Lunayev is the best shot among us; his shooting is simply masterly. The marksman must be skilled in order to hit his target, for the animal's head is quite small. And one must shoot the animal squarely in the head, for otherwise it will swim away; it is very resistant to injury. If you encounter a seal on the ice, it immediately slithers into a water hole and disappears, for it is an excellent swimmer.

I left the tent to inspect the horizon and spotted a polar bear very close by. He raised his head and followed my movements with keen attention. I tried to attract him by feigning fear and hid behind a large block of ice. I thought he would follow me but he turned around and disappeared. We often played hide-and-seek in this way with the "king of the eternal ice," the outcome always being in our favor, and fatal for the bear. If you show no sign of fear when confronting a polar bear, he will generally hesitate for a moment, the three characteristic black dots of his face swinging back and forth like a pendulum, then quite abruptly run off. Polar bears show extreme endurance when they are wounded. I have witnessed cases in which, even with their hind legs broken and their spinal cords injured, they would manage to drag themselves away on their front paws alone. We once found twelve bullets in a carcass, including explosive ones of the type seal hunters use, which shatter bones and tear the flesh as they leave the body, without killing the animal immediately. A bear that is mortally wounded is a very dangerous adversary. Sometimes one may think he is dead, but then as the silent hunter draws near, the bear will grab hold of him and tear the man apart with his last remaining strength. But as a rule the creature is relatively fearful, and a first encounter with man will cause him to retreat immediately. He runs clumsily, but even deep snow cannot stop him. When a female is passing with her cubs, she is extraordinarily cautious and almost never allows herself to wander within range of a hunter. It is strangely moving to see a female loping across thin, fresh ice with her cubs. She practically crawls on her stomach with her legs widespread, and the cubs jump along behind her like frogs. Although they are excellent swimmers and divers, polar bears do not like going into the cold water in winter. One day we saw a bear that was trying to escape from us break the ice, dive in the water, and swim away under the frozen surface. After a short while he broke through the ice from below and poked his head out of the water to see if we were still pursuing him. Then he dived again and continued swimming under the ice. It was only when he was well away from us that he resurfaced.

Neither yesterday nor today was I able to take a sun sight. The plumb line showed that we were heading south-southwest. I also noticed that the leads were contracting and expanding with great regularity, which confirmed my suspicion that the constant motion of the ice pack is due to the tides; but because we are still on the open ocean we cannot really feel their effect.

As the weather had improved by evening, we are preparing our departure. First and foremost we have to dry our clothes, and we are going to sacrifice a sledge and a kayak to dry our wet things in front of the flames. For ten men, three sledges and three kayaks are quite sufficient. We will lash two kayaks together side by side to enable them to withstand any strong waves.

The state of our supplies: In addition to the stocks of bear meat, we have twelve sacks of biscuits, three pounds of salt, and four pounds of dried meat for broth. There are also our warm clothing, our dishes, our skis, and our most valuable belongings of all—the guns and ammunition.

JUNE 5

The weather is changing before our very eyes. A slight southerly breeze has replaced the north wind, and it is overcast and damp. Hidden behind the clouds the sun shines occasionally with a dull glow. This brighter light is again giving us violent attacks of snow blindness. Every object, even a close one, appears blurred as if seen through a muslin curtain; sometimes we even see double.

We are still drifting southward. I have calculated our position to be 81°09′, but I do not trust this to be altogether correct, as one of my eyes does not see well and I cannot clearly distinguish the horizon.

At four in the afternoon, I could see a vague outline to the east-southeast, but I could not determine exactly what it was. Far away on the horizon were two little white clouds with a slight pinkish tinge. They were visible for a long time, never changing shape or position, until the fog finally engulfed them. As I was incapable of explaining what I had seen, I did not say anything to my companions for the time being, in order not to arouse any false hopes.

We have never before crossed such rough terrain, full of pools, channels, and crevasses. A great amount of water sky is visible on the horizon. Flocks of little auks and white gulls fill the sky. The gulls make a terrible racket, screeching all night long, fighting over the remains of our dinner and keeping me awake. They are like evil spirits flitting around us, reveling in our unfortunate circumstances. They laugh, shriek, whistle, and scream like hysterical women. Never shall I forget their strident cries. Nor the torture of the sun, blinding us even at night in our tent through every crack and slit in the canvas.

Today our sounding line again failed to reach bottom, although we lowered it twice. As usual, the line indicated we are drifting south. The wind is again blowing from the north. Hurrah!

JUNE 6

I have just recalculated my figures from yesterday's observation and found them to be exact. We are below 81°01′. During our idle week we have managed to put behind us an entire degree of latitude, that is to say, all of sixty nautical miles. Perhaps this progress is not due to the winds alone; I am convinced that the current also has something to do with it.

Now that we are exactly at latitude 81°, the question of our longitude is even more urgent. I am sure that we are drifting to the west of the Franz Josef archipelago, since

Alexandra Land, according to my map, is farther north than 81°, and we should have reached its northern shore long ago. There are only two possibilities: Either my map is wrong, or we are already between Franz Josef Land and Svalbard. But in the latter case we must have also gone by Gillis Land without even seeing it. I cannot decide which of these suppositions might be correct. Perhaps we shall fail to make landfall on the western edge of Alexandra Land; if so, our hopes of reaching Cape Flora and the Jackson camp with its coveted supplies will vanish. We would then have to try to reach Svalbard. But even before considering all these hypotheses there remains one vital question: Will our strength withstand the hardships that the future still holds in store? Will our sledges and kayaks stand up to more hard use? Will our perseverance and our faith eventually be rewarded? We are drifting endlessly, aimlessly.

Seals keep showing themselves in the leads. They are larger than any we have previously seen, but we have not managed to kill a single one, they are so wary. The hysterical, indefatigable gulls fly around day and night. Today we broke up the fourth kayak and our most delapidated sledge for fuel. We will push on with only three "chariots." We only have a small supply of biscuits left.

JUNE 7

Still in the same position! We seem to be sharing the same fate as Nansen.* We also have our "waiting camp." But what will we gain?

* In June 1895, Nansen and Johansen spent a whole month in one camp, feasting off a bearded seal they had killed, and overhauling their gear.

The same northwesterly wind as yesterday. If it blows more to the east, it will be more to our advantage. The sky is somber and wet snow is falling. On the ice, too, there is a thaw. All around us are nothing but channels and pools of water. It is as if the ice were alive. Water sky is visible on the horizon. Am I hallucinating, or is the ice floe on which we are camped moving faster than the one to the east of us?

Today we shot a seal in the lead, which in everyone's view was larger than any we had killed before. I tried to lift it, and estimated its weight to be at least 160 to 200 pounds. It produced a wonderful soup. Flocks of murres and little auks are growing steadily more numerous. This evening I saw a flock of fifteen flying in a northerly direction. Where are they heading, the idiots? What can they be looking for in this desert of ice?

We lowered the sounding line twice, but did not reach bottom. Again the line slanted northward. It seems there is definitely a constant current here.

Land Ho!

JUNE 9

The wind swings back and forth between the northwest and the west-northwest. Despite the overcast skies, I was able to determine that with no effort on our part we had reached 80°52′ north and 40°20′ east of Greenwich. But I cannot guarantee the exactness of the longitude.

As I have often done, at around nine in the evening I climbed onto a high ice formation to study the horizon. Ordinarily I saw what looked like islands in every direction, but which on closer examination turned out to be either icebergs or clouds. This time, I sighted something quite different on the shimmering horizon. I was so staggered that I sat down on the ice to clean the lenses of my binoculars and rub my eyes. My pulse was racing in great anticipation, and when I fixed my apprehensive gaze once more on the vision that held such promise, I could discern a pale, silver strip with sinuous contours running along the horizon and then disappearing to the left. The right-hand side of this phenomenon was outlined with unusual clarity against the azure of the sky. This whole formation, including its gradations of color, reminded me of a phase of the moon. The left edge seemed to grow slowly paler while the right stood out even more distinctly, like a yellowish line traced along the blue horizon. Four days earlier I had observed a similar phenomenon; but the bad light led me to think that it was a cloud. During the night I returned five times to check on my strange discovery, and each time my original impression was more or less clearly confirmed; the main features of shape and color had certainly not changed. So far, nobody else had noticed this wonderful sight. I had to restrain myself severely from dashing back to the tent and shouting with excitement: "Wake up, everyone, come and see that our prayers have been answered at last and we are about to reach land!" I was then convinced that it was land that I could see, but I wanted to keep my discovery secret, so I contented myself with thinking: "If you others want to see this miracle, you will have to open your eyes." But my companions were as oblivious as ever, and had not even noticed my ill-concealed excitement. Instead of going out and inspecting the horizon, the only way of evaluating our immediate prospects, they either went back to sleep or started to hunt for "game"—as we have named the lice that are regular guests in our malitsi. That seems to be more important to them!

JUNE 10

The morning was beautiful. My hypothetical land stood out even more clearly, its yellowish hue increasingly extraordinary. Its shape was totally different from what I had been expecting as I scanned the horizon over the past two months. Now I could also see, to my left, a few isolated headlands, set quite far back, however, and between them seemed to be glaciers. I wondered idly how far away we were, for my eyes were not at all used to judging such distances. I estimated that there must be fifty or sixty nautical miles to the most distant peaks; how far we might be from the shore could not even be roughly determined: twenty to thirty-five nautical miles, perhaps more, perhaps less. The only certainty was that we were now closer to being rescued than we had been for the last two years. I silently offered up my thanks; but how on earth could we get there?

At around noon I managed to fix our position from the sun. We were crossing latitude 80°52′. Wind from the south. We ate quickly, packed up our belongings, and decided to head for land. By nine o'clock we had covered between two and three miles and made the decision not to pitch the tent until we reached land. Could we do it? The ice floes were in perpetual motion; it was almost impossible to advance without resorting to the kayaks. We spotted quite a few bear tracks; we also succeeded in shooting a seal.

—

Evening has arrived. We sit together in the tent with mixed feelings, for not only have we failed to reach the island, we are now even farther away from it than this morning. The weather is very gloomy; it is snowing and raining, with wind from the south. The surface of the ice was dreadful; my companions call it "glutinous." It was impossible to make any sort of progress today, either on foot or by kayak. Exhausted, soaked through, and famished, we decided to stop and pitch the tent. South wind still blowing. Major efforts have brought us no more than two miles at the most. But we managed to kill a seal, which we are cooking; we have brewed up a very nourishing broth with the seal's blood. Once we really start cooking we do not skimp on the size of the portions. Today we had a good, solid breakfast; at midday a bucketful of soup and just as much tea; in the evening, a pound of meat each, washed down with more tea. Our food supply is ample, for in addition to what I have just mentioned, each man receives a pound of ship's biscuits per day. Our appetites are wolfish! In gloomy moments we are struck by the thought that such voraciousness normally occurs in cases of severe starvation. God protect us from that!

Yesterday I noticed that seven pounds of biscuit had disappeared. This unfortunate discovery forced me to call my companions together and inform them that if it happened again, I would hold all of them responsible and reduce their rations; and if I managed to catch the ignominious thief red-handed, I would shoot him on the spot. However bitter it seems, I must admit there are three or four men in the group with whom I have nothing in common.

Only someone who has experienced such an ordeal can fully understand how impatient I was to reach the island where our two-year odyssey through the Arctic wastes would finally end. Once we reached our landfall, our situation would improve dramatically. We would be able to capture hosts of birds and walruses and we would also be able to take a bath. We have not washed now for two months. Catching a chance glimpse of my face in the sextant's mirror the other day gave me a terrible fright. I am so disfigured that I am unrecognizable, covered as I am with a thick layer of filth. And we all look like this. We have tried to rub off some of this dirt, but without much success. As a result we look even more frightening, almost as if we were tattooed! Our underclothes and outer garments are unspeakable. And since these rags are swarming with "game," I am sure that if we put one of our infested jerseys on the ground, it would crawl away all by itself!

Here is a glimpse of life inside the tent: Everyone is squatting in a circle on the ground; with grim expressions, they are silently absorbed in some serious-looking task. What can these men be doing? Hunting lice! This "pastime" is always reserved for the evening. It is the only possible form of hygiene, since we have neither soap nor water for proper ablutions. And even if we had some water, the fearful cold would prevent us from washing. All too often we have not even had enough water to quench our thirst.

Some of us had originally taken a vow not to wash until we reached land. Who would have suspected that it would be two months before we sighted land? No wonder we all felt the need to indulge in our nightly "hunt." This communal activity united us in a remarkable fashion, and all the squabbles usually ceased during those hours.

In the afternoon I went out with three men on a reconnaissance. Beyond the four leads we will have to cross tomorrow morning, we shall find better going. The ice blocks are unusually dark and dirty, with algae, sand, and even rocks sticking to them. We took a couple of small stones, seaweed, and two small pieces of wood with us, as our first gift from the land—an olive branch, so to speak.

We found a lot of bear tracks. The weather, as usual, is damp and foggy. There is wet snow falling, almost rain. Wind from the south.

JUNE 11

A satisfactory day's march. We covered four miles. Toward evening, we pitched camp on a little ice floe surrounded by pools and brash ice. The morning's northeasterly had by evening become a chilly northerly. The current has pushed us away toward the east, and now our island of salvation appears to be farther south. Good hunting: one seal and a duck. Our eyes are very painful again.

JUNE 12

The wind is still blowing from the north, but the weather is warm and clear. Only the kayak crossings were difficult: We covered scarcely more than a mile. Seven of the men, including myself, are suffering from serious eye inflammation. While crossing one of the open leads we had the serious misfortune of dropping one of our two remaining Remingtons into the sea. It was Lunayev who dropped it, with Smirennikov's assistance. Such negligence made me so angry that I lost my temper and struck out at anybody who crossed my path. This is the second rifle we have lost because of heedless behavior, and anyone who can picture himself in my shoes would surely understand my frustration with such unforgivable carelessness. Now we have just one rifle for which there is abundant ammunition. The smaller repeating rifle is hardly of any use, since there are only eighty cartridges left for it. We still have shells for the shotgun, but it is almost useless against bears, which may be lurking behind every block of ice.

I would have liked to take a sun shot with the sextant, but my eyes were not up to it. The sun seemed to be misty and indistinct and I could not see the horizon at all. According to my companions who can still see clearly, our island is particularly visible today: One can even make out a few details. We saw many eiders in flight that must have come from the island. As our supply of seal meat has run out, for lunch we cooked the bear meat we dried the other day, and in the evening we prepared a soup from the same meat. There is no more sugar, and the tea will last only a few more days.

We are still making little headway trekking over the ice. But we have thought up a new strategy: We work out our course from the top of a rise—that is, we identify the places ahead of time where our kayaks or skis are most likely to get through. Often we are forced to skirt along the edge of a channel on our skis, dragging the sledge-laden kayak behind us on the water. But chunks of disintegrating icebergs, called growlers, often obstruct the boats, and it is not a simple affair to get them moving again. From time to time during our backbreaking toil, one of us sinks through the ice, and that is when we see who can move the fastest. It is imperative to leap out of the icy water, remove one's boots that are rapidly filling up, empty them, and get back to work, all in a matter of seconds!

JUNE 13

The wind has shifted, coming now from the south-southwest. We set off at eight o'clock and traveled, with only an hour's break, until six-thirty in the evening. The end result: about five miles. We had to cross more extensive pack ice that had been eroded by the wave action and covered in deep snow. Crossing a channel we were startled when a bearded seal suddenly bounded out of the water. We also saw a great many ordinary seals but were unable to shoot one.

When the horizon grew lighter, those of us who were not suffering from snow blindness were able to see the island to the southeast. From now on, the tides will probably swirl growlers and brash ice continually along the shores, and we shall be confronted with this repulsive stuff, this ice porridge, all the way to our landfall. Toward evening, the wind from the south-southwest picked up, bringing with it fine hail.

JUNE 14

The same wind persists, with cold, dark weather. We did two and a half miles this morning. On very thin ice, Konrad suddenly broke through a seal's breathing hole that had been drifted over. Totally submerged, he became tangled in his hauling line while the sledge slid forward and covered the hole. We all rushed to his rescue, cut the hauling line, dragged the sledge aside, and pulled Konrad out. He was soaked to the skin and had swallowed some water. We had to pitch the tent right away and light a fire to warm him up.

Our supplies are dwindling. We have only 120 pounds of biscuits left, and our reserves of meat are finished; for lunch we had nothing but biscuit soup, to which we added our last can of condensed milk. The dire state of our supplies forced us to take some quick action, and we decided on some long-term plans that included abandoning the tent and continuing in our nearly empty kayaks. We would be sorry to leave behind nearly all our belongings: axes, harpoons, ski poles, spare skis, warm clothing, footgear, and empy cans. These represent a considerable load, but at the same time how indispensable all such things will be if we have to winter over on these islands. And in all probability, we will not be spared a wintering.

No sooner had we set off again than we came upon some seals and shot two of them. Fortune had smiled upon us once again during our hour of need. This lucky event restored our courage to such a degree that we went back for the tent. The route was dreadful and required great caution; we barely covered one mile.

JUNE 16

We had just pitched the tent when Lunayev brought us the good news that he had shot five seals in the space of an hour. So many animals came close to our camp that we could easily have shot some more, but we had enough meat for the time being.

As far as I could tell from the terrain, we were on a small ice floe surrounded by a jumbled mass of brash ice. There was no way out. Our situation was not to be envied. Moreover, a strong southerly wind had come up that could drive our ice floe away from the island of salvation.

All we could do was wait patiently for the outcome. At least we had the chance to observe a great many seals. Our only hope was a shift in the wind that would consolidate this mushy ice, or would push our floe toward land. Our predicament was quite desperate. It was impossible to abandon the kayaks, or to put on our rucksacks and set off on our skis, since open water would continually impede our progress. Without the kayaks we would be lost. We tried stowing all our belongings on one sledge that eight of us could haul, but the attempt was a total failure. The heavily laden sledge sank so deeply into the snow that it was only with great difficulty that we managed to pull it out. Moreover, it was quite probable that such old sledges were not up to this kind of treatment and would not have lasted even one day. Besides, without the sledges, how would we haul the kayaks? After much reflection I resolved that we must not abandon a single sledge or kayak. I could not possibly take such a risk. Better to proceed slowly than to find ourselves stranded on an ice floe, surrounded by water and unable to escape, doomed, perhaps, never to reach the island that was now so near. Perseverance and confidence alone could save us. Too often we fall prey to impatience. Only seven days have gone by since we first saw the island. At that time we were prepared to endure incredible hardships to reach our goal! How quickly we have succumbed to despair again.

If I remember rightly, Nansen took six entire weeks to reach Hvidtenland, the "White Land." It is true that his situation was a bit less difficult, since he had dogs to help him pull his sledges, and those sledges were much better made; ours were hardly worthy of the name. I refuse to listen to the insidious arguments of the skiers, who are constantly trying to persuade me to abandon the kayaks. I trust my kayaks and I will not give in. I have reminded my companions of my unswerving conviction on more than one occasion.

We set off at six o'clock and covered roughly three miles in the short space of two and a half hours. The bad conditions of the route brought us to a premature halt on a large hummock of old ice. We found some fresh melt-water there for the first time in over a year. No sooner had we put up the tent than Konrad rushed in, overcome with excitement, to inform us that he had found a walrus just behind a ridge of ice. We seized our firearms and ran to the spot. The gigantic animal seemed to be lying motionless on the ice. But although we stalked it with the greatest caution, we did not manage to shoot it. The moment we took aim, it slipped into the water and disappeared at once. As we drew nearer we saw that several animals must have been lying there.

All day long there was a thick fog, which made it impossible to calculate our position.

JUNE 17

A great deal of agitation today. I feel as if I have been struck by a sledgehammer, for I now know that my companions have betrayed me. How am I to recover from such a blow?

Yesterday evening, two of my men (I decline to mention their names) asked to go out scouting at four in the morning. I granted permission and gave them a ration of biscuits, as is usual in these cases. I awoke at three-thirty, roused the two men, and fell asleep again immediately. When I got up for breakfast I learned with consternation that they had not returned. By noon they were still missing. Increasingly worried, I resolved to go and search for them. At first we presumed that the ice had drifted in the meantime, preventing them from finding their way back.

But imagine my indignation when, as we were about to set off, I discovered that they had shamefully robbed us! They had taken a pair of the best boots, belonging to Lunayev; Maximov's warmest clothes; a twenty-pound sack of biscuits; and even our only double-barreled shotgun, with two hundred cartridges. After this dreadful discovery I rushed to my kayak. The thieves had been there too! Twelve boxes of matches, the binoculars, and the soldered tin can containing our correspondence and all my documents were missing. The damned scoundrels had even taken our only pocket watch. Finally I found their shoddy skis left in place of my good ones. In fact, the traitors had equipped themselves impressively at our expense.

I cannot find words to express how appalled and disheartened I was by these deplorable events. The others wanted to set off in hot pursuit of the thieves and mete out swift justice. But after careful thought, I calmed them down by reminding them that the thieves already had too great a head start for us to hope to catch them, and that in any case such a chase would be risky, even under different circumstances. The continual and unpredictable movement of the ice would place us in danger of irrevocably losing our camp and everything it contained. We would quickly lose the fugitives' trail and might be exposed to even greater mishaps. We would be better advised, I told them, to resign ourselves to this painful turn of events, and to reflect on how we should continue our journey. We would have to sacrifice our heavy tent as well as a sledge and a kayak. We might eventually be able to do without the tent, but two kayaks would not carry eight men, only seven at most. Of course, now we had considerably less baggage. So we set off with heavy hearts, four men pulling one sledge and three the other one. I went ahead to look for the best route. When we had covered about two miles, both sledges suddenly broke down at the same time. We repaired one quickly, but the other was far more seriously damaged. We made a stop, while four men headed back to our old campsite and returned two hours later with the jettisoned sledge. We brewed some tea (of which we had found some crumbs among our ammunition) and diligently began to fit the recovered sledge to a kayak and to patch up the damaged one. At ten P.M. we were again under way.

JUNE 18

We continued until three o'clock in the morning and made roughly three miles over a fairly easy route. We moved silently and anxiously through the endless white wilderness, bowed under the crippling awareness of our desperate plight. As we crossed a stretch of water we saw a walrus gazing at us, eyes wide with astonishment.

It grew lighter toward morning and soon the sun broke through the clouds. We had the good fortune of shooting a seal before noon, which provided us with a nourishing soup and some chops. We had covered four miles in all, and decided to set up camp. We made a tent with the sails from our kayaks, by placing our skis on the ground and draping them with the sailcloth that was used to protect the kayaks. In this improvised tent it is warm, light, and airy.

Today we headed toward the south-southeast. At first we came upon some tracks left by the thieves, but very soon they disappeared. Later when I shot an angle on the sun, it seemed to me that in the distance, through the eyeglass of my sextant, I could make out the vague shapes of two individuals. If we caught them now, the trial would be brief: death or mercy? I am not sure, but the others would probably lynch them without hesitation. My innermost feelings also balked at the idea of pardon, for the scoundrels had greatly wronged us, and their shameful act had greatly increased the perils that constantly threatened us. It was because of them that we had had to abandon the big tent, a kayak, and a sledge. How many times had I repeated that I was not forcing anyone to follow me? No one needed to steal away at night, in such a shameful way. In any case I would have been quite prepared to share everything we had equitably, but these unworthy individuals had left on the sly, coldly putting their companions in danger—for they had robbed all of us indiscriminately.

Their fate does not concern me anymore; I would only like to know which direction they took. They must have set off with no particular goal in mind, because neither one of them had the slightest idea of our position, nor of Cape Flora, nor of Svalbard.

JUNE 19

We set off at three o'clock, and traveled until seven, covering the respectable distance of three miles in four hours. Despite the haze on the horizon, we could see the island very clearly. I was now able to estimate the distance that separated us with a fair degree of certainty: eight to ten miles at the most. But my attempts to take a sun sight were not successful. The wind was blowing from the southwest, force 5.

We rested until two in the afternoon, and then continued. The route was good: fresh ice with a little snow, occasionally interrupted by blocks of ice. Moreover, the air was pleasant, even warm. I went ahead of the column to inspect the terrain and pick out the best route. My companions are exhausted from our efforts over the last few days, particularly the crossings. But they are also letting themselves go; their willpower is flagging. How many times have I surprised them, when they thought no one was watching, in the act of halting, resting, or basking in the sunshine? They see these vast expanses of smooth ice and think there will be no more obstacles and no need to hurry. My exhortations arouse little response. They answer calmly: "Why hurry? We'll get there, all in good time."

We called a halt at six o'clock and prepared some supper from seal meat and biscuits.

JUNE 21

I have severe pain in my eyes and can write only with great effort. On June 20 we left at three in the morning and kept going until six-thirty in the evening. The route was very bad in comparison with yesterday, and frequently so difficult that we managed only two and a half miles in spite of all our efforts. During the night there was thick, freezing fog. Then the sky grew lighter and the west coast of the island was clearly visible to the south. My theories that the back-and-forth movement of the ice was due to the tides, and that the southerly winds were driving it away from the island, were certainly correct. But understanding the movements of the ice pack did not make it any easier to travel across it, particularly when the wind was against us as well. The men began to complain about the weight of the kayaks and suggested leaving them behind, taking just what they could carry on their backs. I could not agree to that but once again insisted that everyone was free to make his own decision. I personally had no intention of giving up my kayak and would, if need be, go on patiently as before, with one or two companions.

SUNDAY, JUNE 22

These last few days, there has been no end of squabbling about the kayaks: always the same refrain. The men seem impervious to any form of reasoning, as if they have forgotten that every step brings them closer to the island. There is only a short distance left. It is not the difficulty of the route, the privations, or the hunger that are at the source of their discontent, but simply a kind of mental laziness that is paralyzing their physical efforts. I have again explained my intentions to them, in my calmest tone of voice, and I did not allow myself to be drawn into any sort of discussion. Those who do not wish to accept my decisions are free to go wherever they like.

We set off today with those words ringing in their ears. The route was bearable at first, even if rather heavily crevassed, but later conditions became very rough, with

huge ridges of ice barring our path. Despite these countless obstacles, we managed to cover eight miles today, in
two stages. This forced march brought us so much closer
to the island and now we are filled with the enchanting
hope of reaching land tomorrow evening. This prospect
brought me peace of mind and contentment, feelings impossible to describe.

What is more, the weather has been superb. The sun was
so warm that we had to take off our outer garments and
caps. In the deathly silence, we could clearly see the snow
melting and hear water gurgling and bubbling, trapped beneath the surface of the ice. The sunlight was so strong that
our eyes felt very painful. The island seemed within arm's
reach, bathed in the bright light. No hunting today: There
were no open leads, and in any case there were no seals. All
we saw was a walrus basking in the sun, but it was immediately frightened off as we approached. We have never managed to take these animals by surprise and that is why I fail
to understand Nansen's story about frequently encountering walruses that were so tame and lazy that he had to poke
them with his ski pole to make them move into a position
where they could be photographed.

We continued until eleven-thirty at night, resting for two
hours in the middle of the day. Our only food was the remains of the dried bear meat, spiced with meat extract. We
have only two pounds left. We pitched our tent, hopeful that
we would see all our wishes granted the following day.

JUNE 25

Our rosy dreams of imminent salvation suddenly vanished when, on awakening, we were confronted by a des-

perate situation. One hundred yards ahead of us was the steep frozen wall of a formidable glacier, stretching from west to east as far as the eye could see, roughly ninety feet high, rising almost perpendicular to the sea, of a pure pale blue and as smooth as if it had been sliced through with a knife. Above the wall was the concave, moon-shaped surface that I had noticed long before through my spyglass, and whose enigmatic aspect had always puzzled me.

We had actually reached the western tip of the island on the twenty-third, and only a low-lying cape separated us from it, at a distance of a quarter mile at the most. But an impassable barrier of growlers stopped us short: It was impossible to go on under such conditions. And another problem was the apathy of my companions. The closer we came to the island, the more unbearable their attitude became. They dragged their feet instead of striding bravely forward; they cursed each other constantly and lazed about for long periods on the ground. There was little I could do to rouse them; they remained utterly indifferent to my pleas and seemed to have lost all interest in our future plans. They lay there staring at the sky, and had I not persisted in jolting them out of their immobility they would have been capable of staying twenty-four hours in the same place and in the same state.

The ice that separated us from the island consisted of closely packed floes, but it was very unsafe wherever we looked; we could only proceed slowly and with great caution. The low-lying cape did not have any glaciers. Then suddenly the sea began to heave and the ice started to move. Unfortunately, a fresh southerly wind picked up from the cape and quickly rose into a gale. On vast pack ice there would have been no danger because the wind would have dropped fairly quickly and the ice would have compacted again under the influence of the tides and change in wind direction. But our ice floe was only about twenty-four feet in diameter, and in a matter of seconds the entire situation changed dramatically. A huge gap of at least half a mile suddenly separated us from our companions who were on another floe, and the expanse of water between us grew wider before our very eyes. The gale was driving the ice to the northeast at an alarming speed. As we drifted on the open water now, waves smashed onto our disintegrating ice floe and drenched us with spray. Faced with this imminent danger, we tried to reunite the party by kayaking across the open water, but our efforts were futile. Our kayaks seemed like uncontrollable logs; huge waves swamped them and jagged chunks of ice threatened to pierce their fragile hulls. The cape quickly disappeared from sight and the wave-driven expanse of water grew ever wider from east to west. The wall of the glacier that had only recently been so close had now moved far to the south. We were in a pitiful strait. In our helplessness we could do nothing but wrap ourselves in our sails and seek some comfort in sleep, even though the floe we were crouched on might break up from one moment to the next. We were left to suffer the dark forces of destiny.

Toward evening the gale abated, and at eleven o'clock the tide washed the ice up against the island once again; but we were still eight nautical miles from the low-lying cape. At least our four companions who had been cut off from us previously were able to reach us again. We felt like rats in a trap at that point, besieged by ice floes; the cape, our hope of salvation, had disappeared, and directly in front of us rose the insurmountable wall of the glacier, which not even a monkey could have scaled.

Some biscuits and hot water gave us a modicum of strength after this frightening adventure, but we were all very weak, and no less worried about the depletion of our supplies: All we have left are six pounds of biscuit, half a pound of meat extract, and two pounds of salt. What use will that be to so many people after such a terrible ordeal?

Seals and polar bears have completely disappeared and we cannot bring down any birds, since those scoundrels have deprived us of our only shotgun. This latest complication makes my blood boil. I find myself left to my own devices, for there is nothing to be gained from my comrades. They surrendered long ago!

To crown it all, my health seems to be failing; for several days now I have felt nauseated and am suffering from heart palpitations.

ALEXANDRA LAND

JUNE 28

I had to neglect my diary for two full days because I had neither the time nor the peace and quiet I needed to record my many impressions of the last forty-eight hours. I also had more urgent tasks to perform, as all responsibility rests upon my shoulders.

Thank God our situation has clearly improved. I have just reread my notes written on June 25 and relived the desperate predicament we had found ourselves in. Within sight of salvation, our courage had faltered at the last minute; we became incapable of imagining that ahead of us a door would open to safety, and once we crossed its threshold all our fears would fade like a bad dream.

After that critical evening our circumstances improved, although at the time we had not yet perceived the miracle that had been visited on us.

For here we are, all safe and sound, on the solid ground of an island. What a strange sensation to know that we are out of danger, after spending two years on a heaving ice pack, in storms and cold, threatened by countless perils! And all this is real, it is not a mirage; we can see land, stones, moss! We have been able to calm our hunger pangs and feel more than sated. Twenty-seven big, plump eider ducks are dangling from our skis, waiting to go in the pot. Since we made landfall, two days ago, we have eaten more than two hundred eider eggs, and a plentiful supply of them is piled up nearby. Our hunters are out looking for new bounty and fetching more eggs.

Now I shall relate how it all came about.

On the twenty-fifth, as our situation had suddenly grown much worse and we were so close to despair, I no longer dared hope for any improvement. There remained no other alternative than to try to reach the low-lying cape, roughly five nautical miles to the east, and to force a passage with our kayaks through the savagely broken ice—even though I did not think it possible—or to stay put and inevitably starve to death. I gave our dilemma endless thought.

Then suddenly I had another idea about our possible salvation. I began carefully to inspect the steep, icy wall of the glacier, secretly hoping to find a possible route up it, or to discover what actually lay behind it. And indeed, after a long search, I found, not far away, a passage that might save us.

There was a crack in the ice face about two meters wide, from the top to the bottom of the wall; it did not look recent and had drifted full of snow, not unlike a steep gully. I began cutting steps with an ax and then, for handholds, we rammed harpoons into the ice wall. Our undertaking was successful and we were able to reach the top of this daunting obstacle. With great difficulty we managed to bring our sledges and kayaks to the foot of this improvised ladder and drag them slowly up the glacier along with all our worldly possessions. No sooner was our last kayak safely on the top than the floe we had just left broke up and drifted away from the island. It hardly mattered then, of course, but it had been an extremely close call. One can imagine my feelings as I gazed down on the shifting pack ice to which, only a brief moment before, we had been shackled, utterly at the mercy of its whims! For two years we had been inextricably bound to that white wilderness, to such a degree that there were times when we even forgot how frightening it could be. It was that same ice that had been our last link with the *Saint Anna*, currently two hundred miles away, and two and a half months behind us. Now we were leaving the realm of white death behind for good. No longer ruled by fear, when we gazed from the summit of the ice wall over the vast expanse of frozen ocean, we regarded it in an entirely different light. A miracle had delivered us from that icebound prison, and its mysterious power had been stripped of its terror. Already our years on the ice pack were fading from memory, as if they had somehow been a long dream. For now, despite all our misfortune, we were about to step onto the "land of deliverance."

What a wide horizon was opened to our gaze from the top of the glacier! Near the island one could see open water, but the farther one's eye ranged the less water was visible. Ice ridges and hummocks were lost in the distance and close-packed ice stretched into the horizon. Out there somewhere my companion Bayev had found his grave, searching for his "easy route." Farther yet, the *Saint Anna* lay locked in ice with her thirteen-man crew. The *Saint Anna* would go her way and we would go ours.

On the crest of the glacier wall itself, we prepared a nourishing soup with the rest of our meat extract, ate some biscuits, then hastened toward the cape that emerged from the sea to the west. There was no time to lose, as we had used up all our supplies, and had to rely on the luck of the hunt, something that we could only hope for once we had reached the cape. For on this glacier everything was as dead as on the moon, which in fact it had so closely resembled from afar.

I went ahead on skis with Lunayev, taking only a rifle and some cartridges. I advised the others to follow in our tracks without delay, hauling one kayak and a sledge. I left them with the reminder that any delay would be danger-ous, as we had nothing to eat for the following day. But once again they paid little attention to my orders, al-though there was no way of knowing what unpleasant surprises might still be in store for us.

The surface of the glacier was as smooth as a mirror and covered with snow, permitting the sledge to glide eas-ily across it. I had drawn the men's attention to the dan-gerous crevasses that could be hidden beneath the snow, and had advised them to take great care, and to rope themselves together. I did the same with Lunayev, tying myself to him with 120 feet of rope. In order to probe for hidden crevasses, we removed the baskets at the tips of our ski poles. We moved quickly over the fog-covered glacier, crossing numerous crevasses, fortunately not very wide and therefore not dangerous.

The westward incline of the glacier was barely perceptible. A deathly silence hung over the landscape. The air was still and warm. There were no birds, and we saw no animal tracks on our solitary walk; the comparison of the glacier to the moon was perfect. Suddenly the slope grew steeper and soon the solid ground of the cape was at our feet. Greatly excited, as one can imagine, we accelerated our stride and hurried toward the valley. The spit of land protruding from the end of the cape advanced a good way into the sea, like a stone-covered shoal. There was snow in places, and water flowed into the sea in gurgling streams. We had left the glacier behind; terra firma was ours at last!

Our ears were buzzing, our poor eyes stinging. Our senses and our minds, at this unforgettable moment, were assailed by so many impressions that we thought we were living a fairy tale. And yet it was all true, everything was real! We had land beneath our feet, not shifting, drifting ice. Light and sound danced around us; we saw dappled sunbeams, and marvelous melodies fell on our ears. We often stumbled over stones, sank into swampy ground, or trod across soft and luxuriant moss. The silence of the frozen wilderness, occasionally broken by the strident cries of seagulls, had been replaced by a boisterous cacophony that was a joy to hear. Ringing echoes of Nature in all its exuberance resounded in our ears. We heard the calls of countless birds winging their way overhead, but our snow-blinded eyes were not able to see them. It was a profound chorus, the hymn of life and the hymn of existence. The voices of the different birds united in such a melodious symphony that we almost wondered whether this marvelous concert was really coming from such winged animals.

Gradually, we tried to familiarize ourselves with our fellow creatures, and were soon able to identify a few bird species. There were eiders, gulls, kittiwakes, auks, and many others. Scores of them thronged around the ponds, or flew overhead in dense flocks like clouds, until they vanished in the distance, which our veiled, damaged eyes could barely see. Near the water's edge there was a spot where seals and walruses seemed to be basking on the shore. We crept very cautiously along the beach so as not to frighten them. But our sight had deceived us: As we got nearer, we saw nothing but... huge rocks! We continued to explore our new surroundings. Dazzled by the rays of the sun, we splashed through pools, waded across fords, gazed in wonder at millions of tiny pebbles glistening in the bright light, and marveled over every tangle of seaweed, every clump of moss. And suddenly we spotted some tiny yellow flowers. Flowers! How long had we been deprived of their beauty! And here they were, greeting us again with their pure and charming splendor!

Soon after, a bird flew up from the ground at our feet, as if from within the earth itself. Surprised, we looked around us; it was an eider leaving its nest, in which we found four large eggs, almost as big as goose eggs. What ecstasy! We would certainly not suffer from hunger in this land of plenty. Soon we found dozens of nests nearby. Our overwhelming excitement made us forget all past deprivations and hardships. This little island beyond the Arctic Circle, at 81° north, seemed like paradise to us with all its riches. The sun bathed us in friendly light, and the welcoming birdsong made us feel completely at home.

We continued eastward. Behind us lay the glacier, majestic in a faint veil of mist.

We saw not the slightest trace of our two fugitives! The tide had once again separated the ice from the land, and a vast watery barrier had formed between the two. Lunayev spotted three eiders on the wing. He fired and missed, leaving a hole in the air.

But this shot created a strange echo. Was not that the sound of someone calling? We hesitated a moment, quite astonished. What was it? Were there men living here? There was no doubt about it: A second cry followed the first. Only someone in distress could shout out like that. We strained our eyes and there indeed was a man, running as fast as he could, shouting and waving his cap. As he came nearer, we were flabbergasted to see that he was one of our two thieves. He came up to us, weeping and wailing, begging for forgiveness. He confessed to his wrongdoing and that of his companion, and acknowledged his shameful betrayal. His face expressed such mortal anguish and sincere repentance that we had to avert our eyes. We cast inquiring glances at one another, and then held a brief council to decide what we should do with him. For a moment we trembled in anger as memories of his cowardly act flooded back to us. My inner voice whispered the oath I had taken to "shoot the ignominious thieves on the spot if ever I encountered them." Anger rose up inside me again. Then I took a closer look at the fellow: He was truly pitiful and his pleas went straight to the heart. I thought of the miracle that had delivered us from an icy death and how I had just now so deeply felt the beauty of the earth and of life, like someone brought back from the dead. Swayed by the overwhelming power of such emotions, I decided to pardon the man. Yet had I met him only a few hours earlier, on the ice, I would most certainly have executed him, which alone could expiate his crime.

The poor devil thanked us with tears of joy and threw himself at our feet. When he and his companion had heard the whine of the bullets, which by chance had whizzed by their lair, they thought that the hour of vengeance had arrived, and decided to surrender.

We immediately asked to be led to their "hideout." This was, in fact, just a simple ditch where they had been living like animals. They had lit a fire; all around lay the skins of all the eiders they had eaten, as well as fresh eggs. That is where we found the other thief. He seemed to have guessed we would spare their lives, although they deserved to lose them a thousand times over. We could hardly recognize him, and he must have suffered terribly during his escapade. He looked quite ill, although only nine days had gone by since they left us. When I asked what was wrong, he did not answer. It was obvious that he was in very poor health. Then, as if to reassure me he said, "I will soon be well again. Navigator, sir, I shall never leave you again."

We regained our good mood and high spirits. There was no threat of starving here. There was an abundance of driftwood, and soon a cheerful fire was blazing.

The "troglodytes" invited us to supper and offered us an omelette cooked in duck fat in an enameled pan. Our faithless comrades told us that they had not damaged or destroyed any of the stolen items; all they had eaten were the biscuits. Fortunately the large tin can containing the ship's documents and our correspondence was still in their possession and intact, although they had been very short of containers. We found the omelette to be excellent, even without salt, and we sat for a long time engrossed in animated conversation around the flickering flames.

The thieves told us about their journey: One night they had been very rudely awakened by a polar bear, but they quickly regained their wits and fired at his head, which killed him on the spot. His skull lay near the campfire like a hunting trophy.

An abundance of impressions and thoughts racing through our minds made sleep impossible. We imagined all sorts of plans for the future, working out what we ought to do first.

But we had still seen neither hide nor hair of the other six, who should have joined us long ago with the kayak and the sledge. One of the two delinquents had already climbed up twice onto the glacier to look for the latecomers and guide them to our shelter, but each time he returned alone. It was five o'clock in the morning on June 26 before we finally stretched out on the ground and fell into a light sleep.

At noon, Lunayev and one of the two thieves climbed back up the glacier and came upon the following tableau, a quite idyllic scene, indeed: At the summit of the glacier there was a sledge tied to a kayak, and in the kayak, covered in sails, were the six men, sound asleep, without a care in the world. When awakened, they confessed to having been there since six o'clock the previous evening, in plain sight of the cape, which was practically within reach. But their chronic laziness had stopped them from going any farther. The wind had blown away all my good advice and they had not budged. Nothing could stir them, all they wanted to do was sleep, and they did not seem to care whether there would be anything to eat the next day. They would have stopped even earlier, but the fear of not being found had pushed them this far. At eight o'clock in the morning they had awakened from their long sleep, shared the last biscuits, and lain down again right away. Fortunately, Maximov had remembered to wind the chronometer. They were the epitome of indolence and stupidity. I was not pleased that they had been wakened. It would have been interesting to see how much longer they would have slept, and at what point they would have deemed it necessary to get up, leave the glacier, get to dry land, and think about finding some food! I have often tried, but always in vain, to fathom their thoughts; all I know is that it is extremely aggravating to be involved with characters of this nature in such dangerous circumstances. They are always there, I can see them, but that is all. Often it would be better not to see them, for they are of no help whatsoever; they are, in fact, more of a burden than anything else, and they have ambitions that are totally unwarranted. During the most critical moments I was always essentially alone, and it was then that I understood the profound truth of the precept: "It is when you are alone that you are free. If you want to live, fight for as long as you have strength and determination. You may have no one to help you with your struggle, but you will at least have no one dragging you under. When you are alone, it is always easier to stay afloat."

After devouring the eider meat and the eggs that Lunayev had brought along, my laggards found sufficient strength finally to tackle an energetic task. They set off for the cape, and joined up with us at nine o'clock that evening. When I rebuked them for their laziness, indolence, and lack of conscience in service of a noble ideal, they remained silent at first, and then each of them started to blame his neighbor. Time and time again they had shown a total lack of character, and no sense of duty or responsibility! They seemed to want to compete among themselves to prove who was the most useless.

Early in the morning on June 27, I sent four men up to the glacier to bring back the second sledge and kayak, and I instructed the others to finish setting up camp and to hunt for birds and eggs. As for myself, I set off with the rifle under my arm to scout the area and find out where we were. On my map I could find no landmass that corresponded to the shape and nature of our new locality. I was groping in the dark and longed so much to know more! Toward the south, the ice-free spit of land was part of a larger region that was covered with glaciers. The northern side of the cape was very low, but toward the south there were elevated slopes, and the southern shore itself was a rocky cliff, jutting sixty feet above the waves. The spit of land was roughly twelve to fifteen miles wide. I reached the southern shore after walking for over two hours. There was almost no snow on any of the rocks, and water gushed down into the sea in noisy torrents. What a magnificent scene I had in front of me, with the vast blue ocean stretching to the horizon. Only a few isolated icebergs, well eroded by the sea, drifted here and there. In such splendid natural surroundings, one still expects to see some sign of human life: One's eyes automatically search for the sight of a sailboat or a steamship with its smokestack.

To the east and southeast there was an inlet, free of ice. I was now certain that if, during the critical period of the previous weeks, fog had hidden this island from our sight for even a few days, we would simply have passed it by, and been irresistibly carried out to the open sea on our ice floe, where we all would have perished long before reaching Svalbard.

My thoughts often turn now to the proud *Saint Anna* and those who stayed behind. This is where she should be, safe from danger. Under sail alone, with no assistance from her engines, she would have run well before the waves of this mighty sea.

The icy, biting wind whipping off the glacier almost blew me over, and finally forced me to retreat. On the way back, I shot two more eiders. At noon I cooked up a fine meal of scrambled eggs.

There was no shortage of eggs; I had only to reach out my hand to find one of the countless nests. The hunters returned at the same time, at around five o'clock, with a bounty of thirteen eiders. Konrad and Shpakovsky had made an extraordinary discovery during this outing, for they had pushed as far as the southwestern corner of the island. Near the sea, a heap of stones with a very regular form had caught their attention. When they went closer, they discovered a beer bottle and some patented screw tops. Suspecting it might be a hiding place, they carefully removed the piles of stones and found a tin box containing a Union Jack still in excellent condition. Under the box a note in a bottle gave the following explanation:

> The Jackson-Harmsworth polar expedition landed here on Cape Mary Harmsworth on August 7, 1897, having left Cape Flora the previous day on board the yacht *Windward*. We intend to sail to the northwest, to ascertain whether there is land in that direction and then, if possible, to reach the Johannesen islands. All is well aboard.
>
> *Frederick G. Jackson, Leader of the Expedition.*

I do not know much English, but with the help of a little dictionary I had brought with me, and Nilsen's assistance, we were able to translate the message.

Now all my doubts had been resolved, much sooner than I could have hoped. We are at Cape Harmsworth, the southwestern tip of Alexandra Land. And I also understand why my map only indicates its western and northern coasts with a dotted line. Fortunately, the island's name was written on the map, and its southern coast, so crucial for the next stage of our journey, was also marked.

Today, June 28, our position is 80°35′. Tomorrow we intend to proceed in the direction of the southern coast and continue our journey across land as quickly as possible toward Cape Flora and the camp of the famous English explorer, Frederick Jackson. It seems to me that we are on a well-known and previously traveled route that will lead us right there. Our supplies should last us for five days, which will take us quite far.

The Fateful Journey to
Cape Flora

JUNE 30

We struck camp at Cape Mary Harmsworth yesterday
morning at about nine, to head for the south coast in the
direction of Cape Flora. It was with heavy hearts that we
left behind this hospitable shore; we had really felt at
home here after so many weeks of hardship. If there had
been no hope of finding a comfortable shelter at Cape
Flora, we might have stayed on at this pleasant cape. We
could even have wintered over without fear of undue
hardship.

After two hours, during which we managed to shoot a
few eiders, we reached the south coast. Our two kayaks
had been repaired and now had double canvas covers,
thoroughly impregnated with melted seal fat. My kayak
could now easily carry two men in addition to our supplies, and the other one could take three. We had the op-
tion of all ten of us going on foot along the glacier,
hauling the kayak-laden sledges, or of forming two

groups, one of which would go along the coast on skis, while the other went by kayak from one cape to the next. The latter would be the faster alternative, and offered the possibility of killing a few seals along the way. After careful consideration, we decided to split up and fixed a black cape visible in the distance, which probably borders Weyprecht Bay, as our meeting point. Before setting off, I reminded those on foot to be extremely careful about the numerous crevasses in the glacier. I warned them, in their own interest, against carelessness and distraction. All our belongings were stowed in the two kayaks, so that the skiers had nothing to carry but lightweight rucksacks containing their provisions.

We had no sooner left the water's edge than a walrus attacked us. I quickly fired in his direction and he immediately disappeared under the waves. We made good progress, and those on the glacier did as well; they were visible from the water. We could see them waving their caps at us, striving not to be left behind. Walruses threatened us on several occasions as we paddled toward our destination, so we had to be very careful, and above all to be prepared for the worst, for it was hardly an ideal spot to fend off an attack. We were clearly at a disadvantage, for on the port side rose a sheer face, roughly one hundred feet high, while ahead of us and to starboard was the open sea, with a few ice floes.

We approached the black cape at around eleven at night, but could not land since the bay was still icebound. We set up our camp on the edge of the ice and lit a fire with driftwood we had brought from Cape Harmsworth. In the meantime the skiers arrived. We had covered at least twenty-five miles. If we could continue at that rate, we should reach Cape Flora within four days at the latest. On a number of occasions the skiers had seen bear tracks on the glacier, but no sign of the animals themselves. I regretted having had to sacrifice the third kayak; otherwise we should have been able to lash two kayaks side by side and travel all together by sea, thus avoiding this unsettling separation into two groups.

I have just seen a few more walruses. They often poke their heads out of the water. They are far more repulsive than one might imagine: Their heads and necks form a mass of bloated folds; from their lips and around their muzzles hang long, thick whiskers, which give them a sort of mustache. But strangest of all are their little bloodshot eyes and their astonished and threatening—even aggressive—gazes. Their long tusks give them a prehistoric look, which has earned them the reputation of feeding solely upon human flesh. As they emerge from the water, they puff and blow very noisily, and when you hear such sounds, your hand reaches involuntarily for your rifle. There is no doubt that in open water they are a serious danger for small craft. On the ice they look rather harmless, but their gigantic size is astounding. Meeting a walrus is analogous to encountering an enormous hippopotamus, which would be similarly terrifying on first sight.

In the kayak, I was constantly on the lookout for possible walrus attacks, and I kept a loaded rifle at the ready, attached to the boat by a long rope. I also had an ax within reach, although I was less convinced of its effectiveness against a sudden assault. A walrus in the water is a formidable opponent, particularly when one is in an eleven-foot canvas kayak! Polar bears are hardly friendly creatures, but compared to walruses, they can be considered almost harmless. Thus not all my companions were particularly enthusiastic about traveling by kayak, but it was good, nevertheless, that some of them had the choice.

The landscape around us is fairly monotonous: one glacier after another. From time to time the snow gives way to dark, rocky areas. I find it hard to believe that all of Alexandra Land will have the same monotonous scenery. If this is the case, however, we ought to have renamed Cape Harmsworth "the Promised Land."

JULY 1

Yesterday we set off again at about ten A.M. Most of the men are again letting themselves go, and their omnipresent need for sleep has once again gained the upper hand. I plead with them, cajole them, and give them orders, but with little success. I employ all my eloquence in trying to convince these "lazybones" that we simply must hurry if we do not want to be caught by the south wind that will fill the sea with pack ice, blocking our way. Besides, we have far too little food to be able to stop for long. Had we not, in any case, left Cape Harmsworth well rested and with renewed strength? Delight in good fortune does not last long with these fellows. They never act of their own free will, but merely follow each other like sheep. They hang their heads, every one of them, their faces full of despair.

Arhireyev was the most resistant to continuing. During the last few days, he had reached the point that it was impossible to get him to fetch driftwood for the fire, or water from a nearby stream. Only at the threat that he would receive no lunch or dinner would he get to his feet and grumblingly do what he was told to. He got along with none of his comrades, cursing and snarling at us all.

Lunayev, Gubanov, Smirennikov, Regald, and Arhireyev are on skis, the rest of us in the kayaks. We intend to meet up next at Cape Neale on Prince George Land, which is separated from Alexandra Land by the wide Cambridge Bay. The current is against us now, and we must paddle strongly to keep up with the skiers. Upon arriving at the bay, where the ice was still fairly thick, we hugged the edge of the pack ice to be able to keep the others in sight, in case they encountered some major obstacles. Moreover, the walruses would be a danger if we headed out to more open waters. I raised a sail, which helped us along; the other kayak could not do so as they have no mast: Those foolish sailors had burned it at their useless campsite on the glacier. Such thoughtless acts always come back to haunt one in such uncertain circumstances as these: Their punishment was now having to paddle twice as hard. If they had been brighter, they would have replaced the mast with a ski pole! A west wind is blowing strongly, whipping up some high waves.

We arrived at Cape Neale at ten in the evening and found ourselves in a sheltered bay. The cape is a flat, moss-covered promontory that slopes down to the shore. A multitude of streams gush and splash noisily into the sea. Sheer walls of basalt protect the cape on both sides, one of them terminating in a steep glacier. No sooner had we landed than we heard an infernal clamor, but for a long time we could not determine its source. Shrieking noises seemed to be coming from the top of the rocks, and must have been the cries of birds, as on Cape Harmsworth. But the sound here was much more piercing, and so unbearable that it was actually painful to our ears. It was as if evil spirits were voicing their anger about our intrusion. But we did not manage to catch sight of the creatures themselves, as they remained hidden against the dark background.

The birds were visible only as thick, cloudlike flocks against the blue sky, immense congregations of such density that one could not make out the slightest detail, as if they were distant swarms of buzzing flies. What sort of birds were they? If I was not mistaken, when I looked closely I thought they could have been gulls, murres, little auks, and others. We could have collected a huge number of eggs, but it would have been a risky business; it would have required days of acrobatic climbing to scale the sheer glacier, and it would have been impossible to descend again without ropes.

———

We have been here for two days now, and the other group has not yet arrived. My mind is tormented by the possible causes of this long and inexplicable delay. So close to their goal, had they been overtaken by their chronic need for rest, as on the Worcester Glacier? I am sure they are capable of anything. They had taken their malitsi with them. I sent Maximov and Konrad to look for them. A fresh wind had picked up, driving ice floes toward the bay.

My two envoys came back at six o'clock in the evening, having walked for seven hours without seeing the slightest trace of the missing men. A few hours later, we heard a noise, and there they were, only four of them: Arhireyev was missing!

The new arrivals told us that Arhireyev had been having problems since the previous morning. He was constantly falling behind; sometimes he refused to go any farther, sitting or lying down on the ice. At first his comrades did not trust him, suspecting he was up to one of his old tricks. If they lifted him up and dragged him bodily along, he would walk for a little while, but then he would lie down again, saying, "You can kill me, but I'm not going any farther with you!" When his companions asked him what was the matter, he complained of pain in his lungs and eyes.

Toward evening Arhireyev's legs gave out completely, as if he were paralyzed. He lay motionless, unresponsive to questions, muttering incoherently. It was too difficult to transport him on skis, so his comrades decided to stop for the night. In the morning, Arhireyev could neither move or speak. His comrades sat with him until ten o'clock, when, worried that they would not be able to catch up with us, they left Arhireyev behind and hurried toward Cape Neale. They confessed that on their way they had noticed a great many bear tracks. And it was in these conditions that they had left the poor, helpless fellow! Such brutal behavior exasperated me greatly at first; then I reasoned that it would have been impossible to take the dying man with them, and even we ourselves could not have helped him. However painful the event, we had to accept the inevitable. Nevertheless, after the four of them had taken some comfort in the form of a nourishing soup, I sent them back with a sledge to the place where their comrade lay.

JULY 2

They returned at ten o'clock, announcing that Arhireyev had died during their absence. At first they wanted to carry the body from the ice onto earth; but as the ice was very unstable, they had to abandon that idea.

Since three men are sick, I am obliged to change the teams and send Lunayev, Shpakovsky, and Nilsen off in one of the kayaks; they are suffering from swollen feet and symptoms of scurvy. Konrad and I will be in the other kayak. Now Maximov, Regald, Gubanov, and Smirennikov will be on skis. I entrusted Maximov with the command of this group, and gave him precise instructions in accordance with my map. They were to leave after we did, with one rifle, seventy cartridges, a bucket, and five cooked eiders. The weather is improving; the wind has shifted to the north. We shall rendezvous next at Cape Grant.

JULY 3

We set out at noon. We struggled through the broken pack ice, which had been driven against the shore by the wind, until we reached open water. Our frail craft headed for Cape Grant, fifteen to eighteen miles away. Fortunately, the unfavorable wind did not prevent us from raising our sail. We had replaced the missing mast on the other kayak with some ski poles. The two kayaks moved forward nicely, but the cold, biting wind and sizeable waves made the sailing conditions unpleasant. We often resorted to paddling to keep warm. The walruses paid us three un-welcome visits. Each time we managed to repel their at-tacks. The assailant generally rose up out of the water about 150 feet away, huffing noisily as he observed our movements. Suddenly he would dive and we could see him beneath the water as he turned on his side and headed our way to ram us with his powerful tusks. We quickly laid aside our rifles and raised our paddles to strike the beast, but in each instance he managed to avoid our blows, and eventually moved out of range. It was gen-erally at that point that we would fire a shot, which put an end to his pursuit.

We crossed Grays Bay and were heading for Cape Grant when a violent wind blew up out of the northeast. Together with the current, this wind threatened to carry us out into the open sea. It became obvious that there is a very strong tidal current between Cape Grant and Bell and Mabel Islands. Within only a few minutes, we had drifted four nautical miles from the cape. We had to rapidly furl the sails and paddle with all our might. It was not until about five in the morning that we reached the ice barrier that floated just offshore from the cape. But even during this exhausting incident, we still managed to shoot sixteen diving ducks, which we devoured raw, right then and there, with a bit of salt.

And now all five of us are sitting in the shelter of a very steep, rocky cliff; glaciers descend on either side of us and, as at Cape Neale, there are countless birds' nests.

Although our journey has taken seventeen hours and we have been here for a whole day, we are still waiting for our companions on skis. Soaked to the skin, we cannot seem to dry out in this damp weather. This does nothing to raise our flagging spirits. At dawn, Nilsen and Konrad wanted to take the kayaks to a more sheltered place, but Nilsen started to be blown out to sea, and we had to rush to his rescue in the other kayak.

Nilsen is sick and so lethargic that he seemed to surrender to the current almost without resisting; he did not even paddle as the current swept him away, and, despite the danger, seemed almost indifferent when we came to his rescue. Certainly he has become quite peculiar; he walks unsteadily and often sits silently on his own.

JULY 4

Abominable weather. Strong easterly wind with penetrating cold and snow. We are still patiently waiting for the others to join us. The sky cleared during the night, so that we can now see a rocky island to the east-northeast, which must be Bell Island. The strait that separates it from Prince George Land is not yet free of ice. A second island is now visible a little farther away, most probably Northbrook Island, site of the famous Jackson encampment at Cape Flora. It does not seem possible that we could be that close to our destination, but, according to my map, it can only be Northbrook Island. We are at least twenty-five miles away, and yet it seems so near. The air here is so perfectly clear that the contours of the tall, dark rocks stand out against their surroundings with incredible precision; such conditions ordinarily reduce one's perception of distances by half. Nansen called one of the capes of the Franz Josef archipelago "The Castle" because of its distinctive shape. I fully agree with his description. Most of the headlands I have seen thus far looked indeed very much like castles or cathedrals, particularly the rocks of Bell Island when seen from Cape Grant or a more southerly point. Their slopes and lower cliffs are generally covered with ice or snow, while the ridgelines are crowned with rooflike glaciers. Even from this distance, the rock no longer gave the impression of a shapeless mass, but resembled an immense castle, or a giant, ornately constructed dome. The vertical escarpments of basalt seemed, from afar, to be perfectly regular and of identical height. On these rock palisades, between them, and behind them were thousands of nesting birds.

After careful consideration, I no longer had any doubts that we were very close to the Jackson camp. I would soon find out whether my plan to head for Cape Flora was sensible, or whether all our trials and tribulations, all our efforts and losses, have been in vain. Twenty-two years is a long time.* What will remain of the camp? I was haunted by "ifs" and "buts." What else could we do? Where else could we go? Toward Svalbard, perhaps? Not likely: From Cape Mary Harmsworth I had noted that loose pack ice stretched away to the west, and I knew that we had only two kayaks for ten men.

Would we be capable of such a lengthy detour? My companions no longer had the strength for such a journey, and at present our equipment could barely stand up to our most basic and urgent needs. No sooner had we left the *Saint Anna* than our sledges were already falling apart; now they consist only of fragment and splinters, held to-

---

* By 1914, it had actually been 17 years (not 22) since Jackson had abandoned Cape Flora. Albanov was ignorant of later visitors.

gether with wire and string. Our clothes are nothing but
filthy rags soaked in seal oil and swarming with lice. Our
supplies consist of two pounds of salt.

No, absolutely not! There could be no question of heading for Svalbard, certainly not this year. What if we were to
rest for a while at one of the capes, where there is shelter
and an abundant food supply, as my men have so often suggested? But what would be the use? At best, we could winter over, but still without any hope of erecting a tolerable
building or improving our equipment. It would be a form of
suicide. And winter is so cruel in these latitudes! We would
be living in the rocks, with a walrus pelt for a roof and a
bearskin for a door! Such places are fine for men as strong
as oxen with resolute souls and iron wills—the likes of
Nansen and Johansen—but not for my sickly companions,
with their sluggish souls, so easily disheartened, scarcely
able to undertake a summer trek in relatively favorable
conditions!

No, by instinct I had found the only possible solution.
When we were on the Worcester Glacier, there was only
one viable choice—head as quickly as possible for Cape
Flora! The hopes we have for the future may not be ful-
filled for us all; perhaps the huts we are counting on have
been in ruins for years. But with what is left, we may
be able to build a shelter, and we shall find provisions for
the winter. If everything else runs out, at least we have
some cartridges left. This can be the only practical way of
spending the winter. We will make complete repairs of
our sledges and kayaks; then we will still be able, if necessary, to consider traveling to Svalbard or Novaya Zemlya.

The snowstorm died down by evening. Konrad went

duck hunting, while I climbed up the glacier with Lunayev to watch out for our four lagging comrades. We skied over four miles in the hope of meeting them, but other than those of a bear we found no tracks anywhere. We came back at ten o'clock and resolved, weather permitting, to go on to Bell Island the following day. I can no longer delay, out of consideration for Nilsen, who can hardly stand. Shpakovsky's condition is scarcely more encouraging. And although his feet are also suffering, Lunayev can still stand and is much fitter than the other two.

The fate of our skiers worries me greatly. What can have happened to them this time? Have they not always lagged behind before? Have they not always expressed the desire to stop and linger for quite some time? It is a pity they only half expressed that desire, rather than making an outright decision, which no doubt they had already reached. So often they have put me in a difficult situation and forced me to waste time.

JULY 5

The weather had improved, so we set off for Bell Island at two in the morning. No sooner had we started than the storm picked up again and we were forced to paddle for ten hours through very choppy waves, rallying our last remaining strength. At noon we were still three miles from the island. Exhaustion forced us to halt on the edge of an ice floe. After we had rapidly cooked and eaten our ducks, we stretched out on the ice, wrapped in our reindeer hides and sheltering ourselves from the wind with the help of the sails. We awoke at four in the afternoon and saw to our horror that the ice on which we had paused to rest was not coastal ice, but a great floating ice floe that, in the meantime, had drifted at least six miles from the island. We had no choice other than to try to recover the lost ground by the effort of our paddles and the sweat of our brows. But during our rest the weather had cleared, and we quickly reached the island.

Nilsen is dying: He can hardly move, has lost the power of speech, and mumbles with great difficulty.

Quite near the island, on a huge block of floating ice, we spotted two large walruses and one small one, about the size of a cow. They were basking in the sun and scarcely gave us a glance as we drew near to attack. We lay in wait, hidden behind the ice. It was a very risky undertaking. We dragged our kayaks onto the ice with poor Nilsen in tow. It was the sight of the young walrus that spurred us on. Its flesh is said to be delicious and we wanted to taste it at least once in our lives. It was an unfair combat. Lunayev and I took aim very slowly and carefully, and fired at the same moment. The cub must have been shot on the spot, for where he lay, the ice turned red at once. It would have been a simple affair if we had been dealing only with him. But the other two old walruses immediately entered the fray: One threw himself at our kayak, panting and roaring, while the other, no doubt the mother, promptly pushed the injured calf into the water. In great danger, we retreated on the ice, constantly firing upon the furious animal pursuing us; we then watched them both splashing frantically around the baby, trying to keep him from sinking. The water, red with blood, boiled and foamed. One of the walruses, certainly the male, kept us in sight and again plunged forward to attack us, bellowing ferociously, so we ran farther away. The struggle lasted for five minutes, then suddenly both of them disappeared into the water. We had wasted fifteen rounds and had most foolishly put ourselves in great danger. As we began to paddle back toward the island after this humiliating "battle," we constantly kept a good lookout, convinced that the two walruses would follow us to take revenge on our attack. We anxiously scanned the ocean's surface, in case the monsters suddenly appeared.

We landed on the island at nine in the evening and immediately realized that Nilsen would not last much longer. He could not stand, and had to crawl on his hands and knees. His brain had already stopped functioning, for he no longer responded to us, only staring with a glassy look. We made a makeshift tent out of some sails for our poor, dying companion, and wrapped him in our only blanket. But we were quite aware that our efforts were useless. He would probably not last the night. Danish by birth, he was one of the first to embark on the *Saint Anna* when she was bought in England, even though he did not speak a word of Russian, but after two years on board he had acquired a good command of our language. Since yesterday he appears to have completely forgotten his Russian, but I believe he no longer understands anything at all. I was particularly shaken by his vacant, terrified eyes, the eyes of a man who has lost his reason. When we cooked some bouillon and gave him a cupful he drank half of it, then lay down again. We had no doubt that Nilsen would be dead by morning.

The loss of this brave man and fine sailor affected us all. Lunayev remarked that Nilsen had suffered the same kind of paralysis as Arhireyev and, in both cases, they must have been suffering from the same fatal illness. The others quickly fell asleep, and I took the rifle and climbed up the rocks to look out toward Cape Flora.

SUNDAY, JULY 6

As we expected, Nilsen is no more than a corpse this morning; his sufferings are over and he seems to have died peacefully, without pain. His features were calm. Remarkably, he did not display that terrible yellow hue, that waxen death pallor that makes the face of a corpse so ghastly.

We wrapped the body in the blanket and carried it by sledge as far as the next terrace, roughly 900 feet from the shore, where we laid it in a grave made of stones. No one wept for this man who had accompanied us for months, sharing all our dangers, fatigue, and hardships. It seems we have become totally insensitive; we have seen death so often, it has been our unfailing companion and cannot frighten us anymore. Nilsen had suddenly disappeared. His hopes and everything he had lived for no longer meant a thing.

We, the survivors, had to leave his grave without delay and try to reach Northbrook Island, twelve miles distant, as soon as possible. We dared not succumb to our emotions, pressed as we were by the need for action and our battle against the elements. Had our entire voyage not been a perpetual struggle against death? It was not heartlessness that stifled our sadness; the conditions in which we had been living for so long had simply deadened our sensibilities.

We even regarded the next "candidate," Shpakovsky, with some hostility, mentally assessing: "Will he make it, or will he snuff out first?" One of my companions even shouted at him almost angrily, "Now you lame duck, why are you sitting around? Do you want to join Nilsen? Go on! Get some driftwood! Get a move on!" When Shpakovsky obediently got up and went off, stumbling occasionally, the other man shouted after him, "Don't you dare stumble! Don't you dare!" This was not hostility toward Shpakovsky, who had never done anyone any harm, and the driftwood itself was unimportant. A healthier person was simply rebelling against the illness that had marked a comrade for its target. Those words were simply meant to kindle some energy and bring back the will to survive at any price. The mind must command the limbs and convert itself into a force that controls the body, even if part of that body refuses to obey. Those who let themselves go in these circumstances quickly fall prey to death. There is no way out, other than remaining master of one's body, down to the last muscle. Every temptation must be repressed. When exhaustion tempts one to rest, the legs give up. It is vital not to give in. One must continually urge the mind to victory in its overwhelming struggle against the body. The seductions of lethargy gradually creep in, ready to take over, and that is where the danger lies. I never used to be too concerned with this sort of problem, attributing any inclination toward languor to such things as spending long hours in the kayak, sitting in an uncomfortable position with the legs bent double. After each long and tiring journey by boat, I could feel my blood stop circulating, which sometimes led to a sort of paralysis of the lower limbs. But as soon as I stepped out onto the ice, I would try to revive the feeling in my legs by doing gymnastic exercises, especially lying flat on my back. Even total exhaustion and profound weariness could not sway me from doing these exercises. Normally the exertion would restore the normal circulation, and my feet would obey me again. But for Shpakovsky and Nilsen, this state of fatigue had reached a chronic phase. The evil had spread and did not delay in attacking and affecting their brains, their speech, and their entire nervous systems. Poor Shpakovsky seems to be headed down the same path as Nilsen; his responses are already confused today, but he pretends that he is not aware that anything is wrong, and is undoubtedly speaking as little as possible on purpose.*

In the morning, small flocks of five to eight eiders flew toward the north of Bell Island. Hoping to find eider nests there and learn what we could about Eira Harbor,† we set off in that direction. But we were disappointed and did not find any nests. It was very difficult, moreover, to walk along the shore, which was quite rocky and covered in snow. The eiders prefer building their nests on peaty soil, free of snow. The birds we had seen earlier had probably flown farther north. There was nothing interesting at the harbor. The

---

* Three American experts in neurological medicine consulted by the editors agreed that the symptoms of which Albanov complains throughout his book—weakness or even paralysis in the legs, mental stupor, and troubles with vision—were most likely not the result of scurvy so much as of severe malnutrition producing a deficit of all vitamins. In particular, a shortage of B vitamins—B_{12}, thiamine, nicotinic acid, pyridoxine, and folic acid—probably caused the ailments Albanov reported.

† In 1880, an expedition under the canny navigator Leigh Smith set out in a vessel named the *Eira*, hoping to discover an ice-free corridor between Franz Josef Land and Svalbard. Smith's party wintered over (the first to do so on Franz Josef Land) in the well-sheltered anchorage he named after his boat.

straits between Bell Island and Mabel Island were packed with solid ice. When we returned to our kayaks we saw three walruses swimming nearby, surveying our small craft with particular attention, so we decided to move them as quickly as possible, for fear that the animals would come nearer. There is still no sign of our four companions who disappeared a few days ago. Of the eleven men who left the *Saint Anna*, only eight remain: my three comrades and I, and the four missing men who are no doubt wandering about somewhere on Prince George Land.

JULY 8

We left for Cape Flora at three in the morning. I was in the first kayak with Konrad, while Lunayev went with our ailing companion in the second, which was carrying a lot of equipment that had previously been in my kayak, such as cartridges, my books, and most of the diary notes. As the weather was exceptionally fine, we were counting on an easy crossing. In the beginning we had to zigzag among the ice floes, but later we were able to paddle vigorously and make good progress. Luckily, Mieres Channel, which is about ten miles wide, between Bell and Northbrook Islands (Cape Flora is on Northbrook) was free of ice. Without hesitation, we set a course straight for the cape, which lay clearly visible ahead of us. All we had in the way of food was one raw auk each. Fortunately we had eaten well on the island, since I had no inkling of what was in store for us.

After about two hours on the water, just as we were in the middle of the channel, a strong north wind sprang up and soon increased to hurricane level.

What had begun as an easy crossing had suddenly changed into a battle against the elements, putting both our frail kayaks and their crews in great danger. At the same time, to make things worse, we must have been caught in a tidal current, for we were swept out toward the open sea at an alarming speed. This all happened within a matter of seconds. In a flash the mirror-smooth surface had changed into a foaming, roiling sea, covered in a thick fog, and icebergs had begun to float out from the straits to threaten us. Our miserable little kayaks were tossed up and down like children's toys, swamped by waves, and left to the mercy of a cruel sea, whose rage seemed to well from its very depths. At the same time there arose yet another potentially fatal calamity. Our sledges were lashed crosswise across the bows of our light kayaks, which frequently caused the puny vessels to turn broadside to the pounding seas, threatening to capsize us. Or, if we managed to run before the wind, the weight of the sledges on the bows made the kayaks nosedive dangerously into the waves. And that was not all: The fog and the surrounding icebergs hid the other kayak from our sight, as well as the islands. But what we could see all too clearly was that we were being blown toward the open ocean with frightening speed, much faster than the icebergs were.

It soon became obvious that it was useless to continue this unequal struggle against the storm and the sea, and we decided to try to approach an ice floe and climb onto it if possible. We managed to drift up to an iceberg on the port side, hoist ourselves onto it, and drag our kayak up after us. I could not be sure of the iceberg's draft, so to speak, but it rose roughly twelve feet above the water level. The waves crashed onto our unstable platform with frightening force, but the iceberg stood firm and deflected their power.

We immediately searched for the other kayak, but without success, even from the top of our perch. Nevertheless, to show we were still afloat, we raised a flag from the top of a tall pole, in the hope that Lunayev would catch sight of our signal and reply.

It was impossible to continue our crossing until the storm abated, and as we were exhausted, we decided to get some rest and try to sleep.

The storm raged all around our floating fortress, and it was bitterly cold. Luckily each of us had his malitsa and we pulled them up over our heads without putting our arms in the sleeves. Then we huddled together in a hollow with Konrad's legs up against my back, inside my fur, and mine inside his. We removed our boots and covered ourselves with care, closing all the gaps and pulling our heads down into the malitsi. We were able to keep warm but we found it somewhat difficult to breathe. Because we were so tired we fell asleep at once, and for seven or eight hours were lost in a dreamless slumber.

But our awakening was terrifying. There was a dreadful cracking sound and suddenly we found ourselves in the water. Our double "sleeping bag" filled with water and began to drag us toward the bottom. We struggled desperately to get out of this sheath, which, to our downfall, we had bound up far too well; the lower ends of the fur had been tucked in tightly, and the whole thing was frozen and stiff as a board. We were like two unwanted kittens thrown together in a sack to be drowned.

It was at that instant that I discovered how true it is that moments of extreme danger seem to last an eternity. I do not know for how many seconds we struggled in the water, but it seemed a very long time. During that brief instant, every stage of our journey flashed vividly through my mind with the speed of lightning. I saw the deaths of our three comrades; I saw Lunayev and Shpakovsky carried away in the midst of the storm, and finally myself and Konrad about to be drowned. I can remember exactly what I was thinking: "Who will ever know how we died?" "No one!" I told myself. The idea that no one would ever know how we had fought against these indomitable elements, and that our end would remain a mystery forever, was an unspeakable torture to me. My last ounce of strength rebelled against such an unsung disappearance. And in the midst of this torment I recalled my dream and its prophecy. Had it only been a vain illusion? Impossible! At that precise moment I was suddenly possessed with unknown strength; my feet met Konrad's, and we pushed each other out of our deadly shroud.

Once we were free we found ourselves standing on the lower edge of the iceberg, water up to our chests, while all around us floated reindeer hides, boots, gloves, and a dozen other objects that we hurriedly fished out of the sea. The furs were incredibly heavy, as was the blanket, which we could not pull out of the sea and finally left to the waves. The icy wind was dying down, the storm seemed to be abating; but we were still in the water, our feet were frozen stiff, and we shivered so much that our teeth chattered. And what now? Would we die of cold? That was all I could think of.

But benign Providence once again showed us the way to safety. As if in reply to my anxious question, "What is going to happen now?" our kayak crashed into the water from the top of the iceberg. And it fell perfectly; after all, everything depended on that! If the sailcloth hull had been torn open on a sharp edge of ice, our fate would have been sealed irrevocably. We would have drifted with the iceberg out into the ocean to perish. But now we would have to summon up our last remaining strength. We quickly tossed the objects we had rescued into the kayak, wrung out our jackets and socks, put on those clothes that were the least sodden, and dismantled the sledge in order to stow it on the kayak. Then we rowed with the courage of desperation. We had to get warm again; our survival depended upon it. I realize today that this hard rowing is what saved us.

The fog soon lifted. The sky grew brighter and the islands came into view again. Bell Island was the nearest, the same island we had left behind on the morning of that ill-fated day. It was now eight to ten miles away. We advanced quickly, although a headwind slowed us down. Because we were not using our legs, they were freezing cold. We tried wherever possible to head for the leeward side of the large floes to find shelter from the wind. With a last burst of energy we finally reached Bell Island after having paddled for roughly six hours. As soon as we were on solid shore ice, we ran madly about to get the blood flowing through our stiff frozen legs. But the place where we had landed was exposed to the wind and our efforts were in vain. We tried to warm ourselves by building a bonfire with the remains of our sledge, skis, bandages from our medical kit—in short, anything that would burn. As soon as the flames caught, we wrung out our fur hides and crouched close to the fire. We had been lucky enough to shoot a few diving ducks, which made an excellent soup. The soup went some way toward restoring us, but we were far from dry. During a night of insomnia, feverish tremors racked my body. Konrad did not lie down at all, but ran about incessantly so he would not succumb to the cold.

The next morning brought better weather. The sun broke through the clouds, the wind died down, and the sea grew calmer. But we remained desperate in mind and body. Both of us could not stop shivering, and Konrad's toes were frozen. But we refused to give in to despair. Action alone could save us, and we decided to set off at once for Cape Flora, but not until we had shot a few ducks, for we had no provisions left of any sort.

Cape Flora,
Jackson and Ziegler's Camp

JULY 11

Only now, after all our trials and misadventures, am I becoming myself again. I am sitting in a small, warm hut at Cape Flora on Northbrook Island. There is a fire burning in a cast-iron stove. As hot as it is inside the hut, I suffer from fits of shivering. I have just finished bandaging Konrad's frozen toes.

We now have an abundance of provisions. On the table there is a plate of ship's biscuits. If one steams a biscuit carefully, one can produce bread—real white bread! It is now more than two weeks since we ate even moldy rye biscuits; we haven't seen white biscuits for much longer, since they ran out on board the *Saint Anna*. But I will relate the events in the order in which they occurred:

On the ninth, it must have been around five in the morning when we set off again for Cape Flora. And once more, as on the previous ill-fated attempt, the weather was splendid, but we had learned our terrible lesson and no longer trusted this apparent calm. We chose the narrowest passage for our crossing, and rowed the length of Bell Island toward the north, as far as Mabel Island, in order to avoid crossing the straits, where, as usual, a strong current was running, carrying ice floes and a few icebergs toward the south.

The kayak with Lunayev and Shpakovsky had no doubt disappeared; yet we still nurtured the faint hope that during our sleep on the iceberg, they had managed to reach Cape Flora. They were carrying our only rifle, all the ammunition, part of my diary, and a few documents. All we had left was the double-barreled shotgun with forty shells—a grossly inadequate supply that would not last long. If we reached the cape, we would somehow have to make bows and arrows, traps and snares in order to hunt for food.

I was reminded of the story about a team of Russian seal hunters who had been shipwrecked on one of the many islands of the Svalbard archipelago. They, too, had no weapons. Like the Swiss Family Robinson, they lived for seven years on that island, relatively happy and content. They fed and clothed themselves by hunting with bows and arrows. They built all sorts of traps that they put to good use. They were finally picked up by a ship that happened to call at the island. I thought of this story as we crossed the straits, so poorly armed. If any walruses chose to attack us, the outcome would certainly be disastrous. We might have had some chance of success against a bear, but bitter experience had taught us to avoid walruses at all costs.

Although we put a great effort into our paddling on that fine day, our progress was slow. It was not until nine in the morning that we approached Northbrook Island, whose shores we carefully explored, keeping a sharp lookout for any signs of human settlement. We were driven by the same spirit of determination that we had experienced on the ice pack before we first discovered land; it was therefore not surprising that our imaginations would at times conjure up the mirage of a cabin where there was in fact only a large rock. As we drew nearer to the west coast of the island, we veered to the south and paddled along a stretch of shore where it seemed most promising to land. As we wove our way among the ice floes, we saw a good number of walruses basking in the sun, but, needless to say, we carefully avoided them.

We soon came upon a good landing place, so we made for the shore. Columbus himself, first stepping onto the soil of the New World, could not have been more moved than we were that day as we beached our kayak. After such a terrible journey that had lasted for over three months, we had finally reached our goal! We stood on Cape Flora.

Our stiffened legs would no longer support us, and we had to lie down on the ground. It was fortunate that we arrived no later than we did: We had never felt so exhausted, and our weakness was a cause of great worry. Perhaps some invidious illness was going to strike us down at the last minute, and the fate of Arhireyev and Nilsen still awaited us.

For even if our legs had not refused to obey us, we felt sick and broken. Only an irresistible curiosity managed to bolster our weary spirits. Lying on our backs, we began to rub our legs vigorously and exercised them as best we could. Then, tentatively, we tried jumping up and down while hanging on to the kayak. After a while, our efforts were rewarded. Our legs gradually loosened up and came back to life. Armed with binoculars and shotgun, we set off eagerly in search of the famous Jackson camp, but soon doubts mingled with our hopes: What if we found nothing but ruins?

The entire shoreline was exposed rock, without soil or clay, and formed a vast stretch of land running from east to west. To the north of this barren beach, the island rose in large terraces that ended in a wall of vertical basalt columns like those we had observed on other capes. The shore unfolded ahead of us in a long, undulating line that curved slightly to the left, in such a way that allowed us to take in the entire coastline at a single glance. Above the basalt cliffs, the island appeared to be capped by glaciers. Countless streams tumbled down from the heights toward the sea. The snow had already melted in places that caught the most sun; heather was growing everywhere, and on the slopes we found the same flowers we had seen at Cape Harmsworth. But Nature was more generous here than on the other capes we had visited. Cape Flora certainly lived up to its name.

There was mud and standing water everywhere; the ground was saturated with runoff, and in places it had been eroded and deeply scoured by the rushing water. The rocks were inhabited by scores of birds, whose strident cries were startling after our silent passage across the vast sea. Little gray birds that reminded us of our Russian snipe ran across the ground among the large boulders. The coastline was almost free of ice; only a few blackened, landfast floes were visible here and there.

We hurried our steps, stumbling over stones, but were often forced to stop and rest our legs, which were still quite stiff. As we traveled on, we saw in the distance the vague outline of something that appeared to be made by the hand of man, which soon disappeared behind a large rock. About 300 yards farther, we thought we could see a tall pole behind the boulder. As we drew nearer, we saw that it was not an illusion: The pole became increasingly clear. There could be no more doubt; a very special surprise was in store for us. It could hardly be a tree as there are no trees at Cape Flora. We moved forward, more and more excited. A few yards farther on, a second pole came into sight to the left of the first one, and now we could see something attached to each one.... The mystery would soon be revealed.

It was a cabin, a real house made of logs, with a roof sloping down on one side, and a chimney, and it was intact. Then we discovered, quite nearby, a second cabin, and even a third. This wilderness certainly had no permanent inhabitants, so this had to be a camp. We were so engrossed in the contemplation of these huts that at first we paid no heed to our immediate surroundings, so we were surprised by yet another wonderful discovery only fifty yards away. Hidden in a ravine, stored upside down with its keel up, lay a large Norwegian-style whaleboat in perfect condition. Stowed tidily next to it were oars and other accessories. It all seemed to have been used quite recently, perhaps this year. As quickly as our feeble legs would carry us, we ran to the largest of the three huts, hoping to find it inhabited. We were certain that a door would suddenly open and out would step a Norwegian or

English sailor with a lighted pipe in his hand. This picture was so vivid in our imagination that we were expecting nothing else.

But as soon as we stood before the hut, we had to accept the fact that it was empty. The windows were broken, but all the openings were sealed with boards. The door was ajar, and the entrance was almost completely blocked by dirty, icy snow. The upper part of the hut was in good condition, but the lower timbers lay drifted deep in snow. Our astonishment prevented us at that moment from taking in all the details. Our gaze happened upon a few large crates half buried in the snow in front of the hut. When we opened one of them, we discovered a second crate in galvanized sheet iron. Our knife quickly got the better of the metal, and to our joy we saw that the whole chest was filled with ship's biscuits made from white flour! We ate our fill, then stuffed our pockets with more. For so long such delicious food had only existed in our dreams.

We opened a second crate: more biscuits, but of an even better quality. There were five crates in all, more than likely also filled with the same supplies. We did not open any of the others. Anyone who can picture himself in our situation can imagine our joy. For months we had rationed our supply of biscuits; in the last few weeks we had none left at all, and had been reduced to eating solely the meat of the animals we shot, cooked in salt water without the slightest seasoning. Those who have not had such an experience cannot possibly imagine our delight. There was a time when I attached no importance to bread—when I had an abundant supply. I found it difficult to imagine people suffering from a lack of bread if they had their fill of meat. When I read Nansen's story for the first time, a long time ago now, I had found the passage where he tells of the prodigious joy he felt in finding bread at the Jackson camp to be quite exaggerated. Today, having lived through the same privations, I can endorse Nansen's every word. Together with Johansen he had lived on meat alone during their winter on Jackson Island. I would even go so far as to say it is easier to do without meat than bread. Bread and biscuit are indispensable; they are the basis of one's diet. I know now and forever the true value of bread. And at the risk of repeating myself, I will say that we were as happy as a couple of children to find this huge supply of biscuits. Just imagine it: five whole crates full!

As we looked around after this satisfying discovery, on the wall, next to the door, we noticed a board with an inscription in the Latin alphabet: "Expedition of Lieutenant Sedov, 1913."

So that was it! This was Sedov's camp. But why 1913, when he had set out at the same time as we did, in 1912?*

Above the board hung two cocoa cans, soldered closed and affixed to the wall with a wire. I thought these cans must have contained their mail; perhaps Sedov and his men were expecting a steamer. Almost at the same time I saw another inscription on the wall, this one written in blue pencil: "The first Russian polar expedition led by Lieutenant Sedov arrived at Cape Flora on August 30,

---

* At the same time that Brusilov had set out in 1912, Russian authorities had sent off the *Saint Foka*, under the command of a Lieutenant Sedov, on an attempt to reach the North Pole (even though Robert Peary had allegedly attained the Pole in 1909). See pages 169–171.

1913, and continued toward the Bay of Teplitz on September 2."

I knew that bay, which was off the shore of Prince Rudolf Island. They had undoubtedly been traveling with dogsleds, for otherwise they would not have been able to bring so many crates and provisions this far.

But how could they have built this cabin in four days, and then let it become so run down like this? It was all the more mysterious if one assumed that they came back that same winter or in the following spring and lived here. I glanced inside: It was completely dark and everywhere were chaos and filth. One third of the space from floor to ceiling was packed with dirty ice that encased furniture, rags, cans, dishes, and a number of other objects. We wasted no time looking any closer, and went on to a large shed roughly fifty yards away. It was built with thick planks and consisted of two rooms, but the door and almost the entire roof were missing. The interior was also full of ice, whence emerged crates, boxes, glasses, clothing, large tin cans, barrels, and so on. A green kayak, which must have been very splendid once upon a time, was also half buried in the ice. Next to the large shed was another, smaller shed, already in ruins, where neatly sawn wood had been piled. All around were mud, horse manure, and puddles. And littered about some distance away were crates containing dishes, barrels, oars, torn harnesses, broken sledges, tin cans of food, and other debris.

A few of the cans were rusty or broken open, but the food inside most of them still appeared to be edible.

As we inspected the ruins, it seemed at first almost as though a fire had broken out in the big shed, which had served as a storeroom, and where nearly everything was kept. The "firemen" had apparently rushed in, destroyed the roof and the ceiling, smashed the windows and the door, tossed a large part of the stores away from the flames, broken everything which was in their way, and doused the hangar with water, which immediately turned into ice. Then after this "rescue" they appeared to have departed the encampment, quite satisfied with their efforts.

But in fact there had been no fire: The walls and the remains of the ceiling had not been blackened by smoke. No, something other than fire had caused this destruction. And it was obvious that these buildings had been fairly recently built. When we opened a few of the tin cans, we found pork and rabbit meat, and smoked and marinated herring. We sampled them without further ado: Their contents were as fresh as if they had just arrived from the finest delicatessen.

We continued our inspection and took a few cans with us. Soon we were standing in front of an odd, octagonal-shaped building, with walls leaning somewhat toward the interior, and a conical roof like that of a tent, rather similar to the outside of a circus tent. The inner walls were covered with canvas and there were bunks built into the sides. Surely such an edifice was not meant for the polar region; it must have been an attractive building before it was relegated to the far North. Here, too, everything was full of ice, from which protruded the top half of what must have been an iron stove. Scattered across the bunks were torn clothes, pieces of furniture, and other sundry items. However, we did make one precious find, when we uncovered a box full of lead cartridges and twelve-gauge shotgun shells that were a perfect match for our shotgun. This "gift" was very timely and it was perhaps our best discovery yet.

On one of the bunks stood a medicine chest with first-aid supplies in a finely polished cabinet, the best-preserved object of all. We were delighted with this find, primarily because of the peppermint drops that would go very nicely with our tea!

Between the shore and the buildings was a veritable rubbish dump, with empty cans flung here and there along with plates, saucepans, frying pans, teapots, spoons, and other things, almost all of them broken and dirty. On closer inspection, we did manage to find a few articles we could use. There was also a huge pile of broken sledges, skis, harnesses for dogs and horses, etc. A secondhand or antique dealer would have found several bargains here, for there was a bit of everything one could ever want. We were agog at the sight of all the treasures that had been piled up here. In fact, this good fortune transported us from a state of extreme penury to unimaginable riches, and instantly supplied us with not only basic necessities, but even some "luxury goods." But one essential item was missing, namely a shelter. Neither the main building, nor the big storage shed, nor the "circus tent" was inhabitable, at least not until we cleared them of ice and gave them a thorough cleaning.

But then, opposite the main building and near a rock face, we discovered a fourth building that must have been put together with prefabricated elements; it was surrounded by bamboo poles sunk into the ground and bound with wire, which made a sort of fence whose gaps had been stuffed with pieces of peat or moss. But the stuffing had gradually fallen out and only the lower half was in good condition. The bamboo had no doubt initially served as surveyors' rods, for their ends still bore typical small pennants. This little construction looked most appealing, for it was neither damp nor dirty; it was situated on a promontory and was far less dilapidated than the other buildings. So it was with great expectations that we went inside. The vestibule contained a little forge, the bellows of which were of an unfamiliar design to me. Beyond the vestibule, the inner door was closed. A horseshoe, a favorite good luck charm in many countries, crowned the door frame. As soon as we entered, we realized that we could quite happily live there. To the left of the entrance was a cast-iron stove with a big crate full of split firewood; to the right was a table, and directly opposite, a wide bunk. Nor were any of the necessary furniture, lamps, or dishes missing. Here, too, the floor was covered in ice, but far less than elsewhere. We decided to move in at once, and put our "purchases" of biscuits and cans down on the table. Soon a cheerful wood fire was crackling in the stove, making the room warm enough for us to dry out our clothes, which were still sodden from our recent, unwelcome plunge in the ocean. Then without further delay we began to prepare what would be a banquet. The rich, fatty tinned meat had the place of honor, and to it we added some dried potatoes that we had discovered upon first entering the building; at last, after so many months, we had a dinner worthy of the name. One hardly need mention that we were certainly not lacking in appetite! For dessert we had biscuits. And what a pleasure to get undressed in a warm place! We felt at home; we had everything we could wish for in such an alien landscape. Cape Flora had brought us even more than we could have dared to imagine in our wildest dreams.

After so many adventures and disasters, we were completely exhausted. But now we could stretch out comfortably, in a way we had almost forgotten. Our torments were now behind us. Had we really suffered such hardships out there in the ice and snow, in our miserable kayak in the middle of the cruel sea, with nothing to drink or keep us warm? Or had it all been a nightmare?

But the memory of our lost comrades intruded on our happiness. What had become of them? Would they ever return? This thought kept us from sleep despite our extreme exhaustion: Where could they possibly be at this hour?

Preparing to Winter Over
at Cape Flora

After a very long sleep, we awoke as if from the dead, had breakfast, and set to work. There was a great deal to do. The most important task was to bring our kayak as close to the camp as possible, and carry our last remaining belongings to our new refuge. There was not a great deal to carry: compass, binoculars, chronometer, sextant, ax, two books, sails, a few boxes of matches, and two or three cans, one of which contained the mail from our comrades aboard the *Saint Anna.* Then we had to organize the supplies that were strewn about everywhere, both inside and outside the buildings, buried in the mud and under piles of rubbish. We did not worry about the cans that were stuck in the ice, for there could be no better place to store them.

But soon we had to accept the fact that over half of the supplies could no longer be used. Many tin cans were rusted through or punctured, so their contents were ruined. We finally took those that were still in good condition into our dry living quarters to sort them. If we could find a suitable space, we could stack them on shelves in an orderly fashion, as in a real warehouse.

Once that was done, we dug out the crates and boxes buried in the ice. It was like digging up the ruins at Pompeii!

Each crate was brought to the cabin and emptied. We worked with the ax and knives and found a great many more items that were ample compensation for our troubles, and brought us great comfort. What did we not find! We could have held a bona fide exhibition, which would have been a credit to the organizer of the previous expedition. We had pemmican, beef, mutton, pork, rabbit, fish of all kinds, dried vegetables, potatoes, large cakes of unsweetened chocolate, powdered eggs, butter and sausage in sealed cans, etc. But many items had spoiled, even though they had lain in solid ice, which proves that they had gone bad at a much earlier date, that is to say, prior to 1914.

We also found a good reserve of tea ensconced in the ice, in half-pound cans. But nearly all of it was moldy and undrinkable. We were able to rescue only a few of the less damaged boxes. As for the tea we did manage to salvage, after having dried it out in our warm "parlor," we were able to make it into quite an acceptable beverage. Much larger cans contained several kilos of coffee, but unfortunately nearly all of it had gone bad. The largest tin receptacles contained oats that, although damp, could nevertheless be used for cooking. It made such delicious porridge that we decided to save the rest of it for winter. Our excavations revealed a few more crates of biscuits that had turned into a soggy mash, an enormous reserve of kerosene, and a box of candles. All of that would be very useful in winter and would help us endure the hardest months. We also found rags of clothing and remains of lightweight silk tents embroidered in red silk with the words "Ziegler Expedition to the North Pole." These words were written, embroidered, and printed on many other objects as well, such as axes, skis, shovels, a kayak, and the portable stoves designed for sledge expeditions, and so on. Everything was numbered and of the highest quality. But whoever Ziegler was remained a mystery to me.*

As I have mentioned, we thought that we were at Sedov's camp and not at Jackson's winter quarters. We were astonished, it is true, to find such disorder, with the buildings in such bad condition, but we supposed that after spending the winter there, Sedov had hurriedly departed, leaving everything just as it was. Knowing that he had left Arkhangel'sk in 1912, we imagined that his ship must have come back for the crew who had stayed behind. The tin cans nailed to the wall of the big cabin must have contained mail for the ship, or so I imagined. But all my other discoveries now made me wonder if I was right, since with the exception of those cans and a few supplies, there was little to prove that Sedov had been here.

One day we began to dig in the ice inside the dirty ruins of the big cabin to see what we could find. On the wall, between the bunks, we noticed some shreds of dirty, mildewed cloth. We could not see clearly in the gloomy

---

* William Ziegler was a rich American industrialist who equipped two polar expeditions (the most recent occurring from 1902 to 1905) that stopped over at Cape Flora. Neither was successful in reaching the North Pole.

interior, but when we carried our find out into the daylight, we saw it was a piece of faded green cloth, which
reminded me that in Nansen's description of Jackson's
camp, he wrote of green cloth covering the walls. He had
also written that there was an iron stove, above which
were suspended some wooden poles for drying clothes. In
fact, everything was as Nansen had described it, and I realized that the camp was not as recent as I had supposed.
This was indeed Jackson's camp! But what a camp. Jackson
had left it pleasant and comfortable with "a lot of room,"
as he described it to Nansen when he met him. They were
quite a small party in his time. Now there were three
bunks in each cubicle, and it was possible to accommodate thirty-five to forty people. Everywhere there were
passageways, corners, and darkness. It was a fine dwelling,
and yet a seedy one. The bunks had clearly been hastily
improvised, for the planks had been poorly planed; the
mattresses were so putrid that we had to dig them out
with a spade. There was also an armchair that must have
once been very handsome, and a desk whose missing base
had been replaced by a rough board. Tin gutters ran the
length of the ceiling to catch the water, and above the
bunks there were shelves for personal belongings. Here
and there lay pharmaceutical jars, visibly used. I became
increasingly convinced that Jackson would never have
lived in such a filthy and neglected place. Can you imagine it? Apparently he was a gentleman who always dressed
for dinner! Others must have lived here since Jackson's
time, and there must have been several waves of occu-
pants. It was once a delightful haven, equipped with every
imaginable convenience, its walls covered with thick

green drapes to keep out the cold. Nansen's story proves that he had found the house in perfect condition. Then a larger group must have arrived late in the season and hastily set up their winter quarters. It must have been at this time that the three-tiered bunks and the gutters were installed, for the roof must already have been leaking. These men must have brought horses with them as well, for we had unearthed several skulls and skeletons. A few of the sledges were designed to be horse-drawn; we later found a number of halters and bridles.

I cannot believe that Sedov could have caused such devastation during his short stay. It would have taken more time to do such damage. There must have been an earlier expedition that left again as quickly as it had come, without taking the slightest trouble to leave the living quarters in good order. Doors and windows had not even been closed properly. Could it have been this Ziegler expedition, which I had never heard of?

I then discovered a large sheet of paper with comical drawings for a New Year's Eve party, which gave me a few clues. The first picture represented two gentlemen drinking whiskey; below this was a caption that we imagined might read: "It'll soon be time to go and discover the Pole.—Absolutely, what a good idea!" The second picture showed a ship that must have been coming to fetch these people, but was wrecked on a reef on the way. The stern of the sinking ship was visible above the water. The third drawing depicted the rescued crew making their way southward in horse-drawn sleighs and dogsleds, perhaps toward Cape Flora. Finally, a portrait of the entire group shows their repatriation by railroad to civilization, after their "exploits." These globetrotters have long since been safe and sound at home with their loved ones, regaling them with the most amazing stories of their expedition.

We also found another empty barrel, which had originally contained wine, on which the words "North Pole" were branded. Its contents were undoubtedly reserved for celebrating the team's arrival at the Pole. In short, we hardly had a good impression of these people, who had left such a rubbish dump behind them, the leftovers of a "bazaar" that contained everything under the sun. Often when something was lacking in our hut, we would jokingly say, "Let's go to Ziegler's, we'll find exactly what we're looking for." This was usually true and we rarely came back empty-handed. For example, "Alexander [Konrad], go over to Ziegler's and find me a sieve for the oats!" Off he would go and find one. That is how we acquired a coffee grinder, a lamp in working order, cutlery, various tools, dishes, and so on.

One day as I was walking to the east, I spotted a tall, narrow stone behind a large boulder. Drawing nearer, I found it was an obelisk bearing an inscription engraved in golden letters: "*Stella Polare:* in memory of those who died during the sledge expedition of 1900."*

It is possible, therefore, that this expedition, too, had left some of its supplies behind.

Finally, we found an anonymous tomb decorated with a wooden cross, painted in red. This burial place was cer-

---

* The *Stella Polare* was under the command of the Duke of Abruzzi, whose expedition stopped at Cape Flora while attempting to reach the North Pole. Abruzzi's sledge team, led by an Italian naval officer named Umberto Cagni, surpassed Nansen's record of "farthest north" by twenty-three miles, but three men died of starvation along the way.

tainly better than the one we had made for our poor Nilsen.

After having inspected and sorted all the supplies, we carried them into the big cabin to store them properly. This storeroom was really quite impressive in the end, and could have been called, without exaggeration, a first-class delicatessen. Konrad had to do most of the tedious sorting and stock taking on his own, for since our arrival here my health had been deteriorating by the day. Shivers and fever racked my whole body, and at one point I was so low and delirious that I did not know where I was, or so Konrad later told me. I also had persistent nightmares and imagined that there were three of us on the island. During these mild hallucinations I would get up and hurry over to my sole companion, busy with his excavations, and ask about our third comrade without even knowing who it might be. The fresh air did me good, often bringing me back to my senses and reminding me that there were only two of us. But this reality would send me into a deep fit of melancholy that would in turn drive me back inside the hut. In addition to this mental torment, I was now afflicted with another ailment which worried me greatly. My legs were becoming more and more swollen each day and were very painful. Konrad was also suffering from the same symptoms. Moreover, the sad fate of our lost companions caused us perpetual anxiety.

When I was well enough, we sat before the door of our "mansion" gazing out toward the open sea. We desperately searched the waves for some sign of our friends. Anything that moved on the horizon became a kayak, miraculously bringing them safely to us. And we would take the binoculars and painstakingly scrutinize each ice floe, always in vain. Colonies of walruses, couched in silent contemplation, drifted past on the floating ice—sometimes heading west, sometimes heading east—content to be borne along aimlessly by the tides.

JULY 15

At dawn, Konrad decided to go to Bell Island. If the ice was not broken up in the channel separating it from Prince George Land, he would try to push as far as Cape Grant to look for the missing men. I could not go with him, as I could hardly stand on my own two feet. No doubt he was afraid I might die and leave him completely alone. Perhaps that was the real motive for his expedition. He took some supplies with him, as well as the double-barreled shotgun with ammunition, and set sail on a fine day with a good wind.

Thus I remained alone, and the hours were difficult. The solitude oppressed me more than ever. I had feverish dreams that brought back memories of all the terrible events of our odyssey, making them seem even worse than they had been in reality; one nightmare followed the next. At times I thought I could hear voices outside, and someone trying to open the door. A victim of my deranged imagination, I leapt off my mattress in terror and went outside to have a look. The fresh air restored my wits for a short time, but the moment I thought of my isolation, a feverish despair would overcome me once more. On the table next to my bed, the loyal Konrad had laid out tins of food and quinine tablets, as well as drinking water. But I had no appetite and only rarely managed to swallow some liquid with a bit of quinine. Then I threw a few logs into the stove and hurried to lie down again, aching all over.

After two full days, Konrad had still not returned, and I was tormented by the thought that something might have happened to him. On the evening of the seventeenth, I put on my malitsa and sat in front of the door to wait. The incessant uproar of birds from the cliffs was interrupted occasionally by a wild howling. Such a symphony could hardly have failed to depress even those who were in perfect health; now, it only deepened my melancholy. Cascades roared down from the rocky heights above me. The snowmelt eroded the snow pack and the glacial seracs, unleashing immense avalanches that crashed down with a fearful sound. These sounds were especially sinister at night, and brought to mind a witches' Sabbath. Their rumblings sounded so near that I got up almost every night to go to the door and make sure the encampment was still standing.

I stayed awake, waiting for Alexander. At around four in the morning I saw, in the direction of Bell Island, a blurry speck moving across the water. Could it be his boat? The ice was drifting slowly southward, which made the black speck look as if it was heading north. Finally I saw something flashing on either side of the speck, in a rhythmical movement, with regular pauses. There could be no doubt! It was a kayak, with the splashing of his double-bladed paddle sparkling in the sun. An hour later he disappeared behind a promontory, then at six o'clock I could see Alexander walking along the shore. I went to meet him.

He was alone. When he greeted me, he could not contain himself and began to sob; he had found nothing. It had been impossible for him to go as far as Cape Grant because of the floating ice, but he could see it with the binoculars, and had given every imaginable sign of life: shouting, firing shots, gesticulating. And he had spent all night within sight of the cape . . . but nothing.

Yet we clung to one last hope, and decided we would undertake a second search together, once our winter quarters were ready.

We could not spend the winter in the little hut, for it was too cold and exposed. We had to resign ourselves to the enormous task of repairing the main cabin. We started the very next day. To begin with, we had to remove the boards covering the door and windows and discard everything that was useless or broken. We dismantled the bunks, since the walls had to remain bare. A good fire would get the better of the damp. We decided to leave the stove where it was, but soon found out that it did not work, so we dismantled it and built a new one out of some bricks. It would thus have the twofold advantage of retaining the heat and being easier to cook on. We had all the necessary material as well as the craftsman, Alexander himself, who had worked as a stove fitter before signing on to the expedition. But we still had to repair the ceiling and the roof, using turf and moss, of which there was an ample supply. There was also much reindeer lichen, dating no doubt from Jackson's time; it seems he had even planned to raise reindeer. Every day we worked from seven in the morning until evening, stopping only for a brief pause at noon, and for tea.

We also made some more discoveries: For example, underneath one of the cubicles we came across over a thousand cartridges for a Ziegler rifle that we had found earlier, and which we hoped to put into working order.

We had already received three visits from bears, but had not managed to shoot one. They were extremely cautious and stayed out of range. They fled as soon as they saw us, diving into the water and only resurfacing long after. And yet their meat was as vital to us as daily bread, for winter was approaching and even the most perfect canned food could not replace fresh meat forever. In addition, our clothes urgently needed repair, and bearskins would be ideal for the pupose. The walruses would have been just as good, because of their blubber and hides, but we would have needed a good long-range firearm.

We collected all the scraps of clothing and reindeer hides we could lay our hands on, which we then dried out on the roof to use later for repairing our ragged clothes. For we were envisioning setting up a real little tailor's shop, for which Ziegler would provide needles, thread, and scissors. We planned to make new underwear out of old sails and some damaged cloth from Ziegler's reserves; this project would occupy our winter days and we would begin as soon as we returned from our expedition to Cape Grant.

Among the debris we pulled out of the big cabin, Konrad found a Russian tobacco pouch, lost no doubt by one of Sedov's men. This brought us great pleasure, as recently we had been smoking every possible kind of ersatz tobacco, even seaweed stuffing from old mildewed mattresses. The last real tobacco we had smoked was on board the *Saint Anna,* at least a year earlier. Since we lacked a pipe with which to inhale our lucky find, we rolled a cigarette out of paper, and very soon small blue clouds rose in the air. Only those who have known what it means to do without can imagine our delight; indeed, we even felt slightly dizzy.

As we went about our menial tasks on the evenings that followed, we dreamed up all manner of plans for the future.

But here is a little tale that will illustrate how enfeebled our minds were at that stage.

The first sight of Sedov's inscriptions and the two metal mail tins nailed to the big cabin had convinced me, for no apparent reason, that a ship from Arkhangel'sk would arrive some time this year. This idea had become so firmly anchored in my mind that I really expected the ship to arrive in August. I even began to invent plausible motives for the imaginary steamer's delay. Unexpected pack ice, I concluded, might well oblige the party to postpone their journey until the following year. To prepare for this eventuality, we repaired the big cabin, prepared all sorts of provisions, and mended our worn clothes. As we could see open sea stretching ahead for ninety nautical miles, we were convinced that to the south there could hardly be any ice, and a vessel could reach us without too much difficulty. It is interesting, from a psychological point of view, that my conviction was founded on nothing at all, but was so deeply rooted that I felt it was totally pointless to open the above-mentioned postal boxes and examine their contents. Those letters would, of course, have provided me with valuable information, and today, now that my thoughts are clear, I am as greatly astonished at my oversight as the next person. How many times did I walk past those tin letter boxes without even giving them a second glance! And yet I congratulate myself on not having read their contents, which no doubt would have altered all my plans and might even have put us in mortal danger—as we shall soon see.

In short, we patiently awaited the next stage of our adventures. We had almost finished the tedious cleaning up of the main cabin. All that was left was to have a housewarming celebration, and to keep a fire burning in our tiled stove to thoroughly dry the place out.

Ship Ahoy!

On July 20, at about six in the evening, with my daily chores over, I set off to prepare some supper in our "mansion." Konrad had stayed behind to finish a job in the big cabin. I paused for a few moments in the fresh air, which always did me a lot of good after a day spent in the damp, stuffy air of the cabin. I let my gaze wander out to sea, without the nostalgia that ordinarily beset me when outdoors. The weather was calm and warm, with a slight mist. As nearly always, ice floes of all shapes and sizes were drifting along the coast, some of them carrying motionless walruses. For once, my desire to hunt was keener than usual, and I was about to return for my gun and alert Konrad, when a strange apparition caught my attention.... Was it yet another hallucination? No, it was real! I could perfectly well see two masts rising above the sea, one higher than the other: a main mast without a topmast, a mizzen, and between the two, a smokestack, trailing a thin cloud of vapor. The hull was hidden in the mist and still indistinct. It must have been about two nautical miles off-shore. As soon as I realized that it was not a mirage, I stood stock-still, my pulse racing.

When I had recovered from my stupor and found my voice, I shouted at the top of my lungs: "Alexander, a ship! There's a ship coming!" Soon the hull emerged from the mist and I recognized the *Saint Foka,* which I had often seen in the port of Arkhangel'sk, while it was being fitted out to take Sedov to the North. At first Alexander must have thought that I was still delirious, for he stared at me warily. I pointed to the ship that was now almost station-ary, obviously searching for a safe lead through the ice to the coast. She gathered way again very slowly, but we could tell that the captain was about to drop anchor. What other purpose could he have? Plainly, he had come back for Sedov, whom he had left here a year earlier. We im-mediately climbed onto the roof of the big cabin, hoisted the flag we had brought with us from the *Saint Anna,* and fired off a few shots. In my agitation I fired two shots from the double-barreled shotgun simultaneously and wounded the index finger of my right hand, but I paid no heed to my injury and continued firing.

One might wonder why the arrival of the ship had such an effect upon us, since we had been counting on it. I can only say that we had not expected it until August, when it would have been easier to sail through these regions. Our joy at this premature event was quite understandable: It brought us the certainty of immediate rescue and our re-turn home.

The ship did not immediately notice our signals, nor did she hear our shots. The fog grew thicker, and hid the

Saint Foka from sight. But there was no doubt that she was about to drop anchor, so we rushed to the "mansion" to get ready for our first encounter with civilized people, not wanting them to see us in our filthy rags. Our "Sunday clothes" were already drying on the rocks in front of the house; we had boiled them over and over again with ashes. Now we had to shake all the dead lice out of them, wash ourselves well with Ziegler's soap, and quickly get dressed. This was done at top speed, and we finally looked as presentable as was possible under the circumstances. We had even cleaned and oiled our boots, although in a drawing room we still would have stuck out like sore thumbs.

Now that we were decent, we went down to the shore, to paddle the kayak out to the ship through the thick and persistent fog. As we paddled out, I started to hear the voices of the crew and the barking of dogs; already the outline of the ship was becoming clearer. Finally they caught sight of us. I waved my cap in greeting. Everyone rushed on deck and stared at us with great surprise, then they waved their caps and a great cheer went up. Faces lit up with joy. Their welcome touched me deeply, although I was still rather dazed by the recent turn of events. But I realized they might be taking me for Sedov or one of his companions, so I hastily shouted back, "Gentlemen, Sedov has not yet arrived." But this news seemed to have no effect upon them, so I went on to explain; "I am the navigator Albanov, from the Brusilov expedition. I left the *Saint Anna* three months ago and managed to reach Cape Flora." The reply was a unanimous shout of admiration and a new round of still louder cheering. I asked if they

were carrying any mail for the *Saint Anna* but I do not rec-
ollect why I asked this question. I then learned that the
Saint Foka had not sailed from Arkhangel'sk, as I had supposed, but Hooker Island, where Sedov had wintered
over, thirty miles to the northeast of Cape Flora. I also
learned that Sedov had died during his trek to the Pole
and was buried on Prince Rudolf Island; that their ship,
like us, had been at sea for two years; and that they had no
fresh news of the outside world.

I had been carrying on this conversation as we paddled
alongside the slowly moving ship. Suddenly I was startled
by loud cries: "Watch out! There's a walrus right behind
you. Climb on board!" At the same moment several shots
rang out. I turned around in time to see one of those vi-
cious beasts trying to attack our kayak. Several more shots
put an end to his pursuit and sent him under the waves.
The *Saint Foka* had dropped anchor by then, so I clam-
bered on board and greeted the crew. We embraced one
another and everyone spoke at once. We exchanged the
basic outlines of our adventures. I learned, among other
things, that from his winter quarters on Novaya Zemlya,
Sedov had requested a fast shipment of coal to be shipped
from St. Petersburg, and so the crew had thought at first
that I was the captain or navigator of the much-awaited
coaler.

The *Saint Foka* was presently out of fuel for her engines. In order to fire her boilers and motor away from
Hooker Island, they had been obliged to sacrifice the
steerage deck and a number of bulkheads: in short, anything that was not indispensable. Even the walruses they
shot were fed to the boilers. When I had first spotted the

ship, they were slowing down because of lack of fuel, and were waiting while other parts of the vessel were being broken up to stoke the fires.

They were calling at Cape Flora only in order to demolish the cabin and shed that we had gone to such trouble to clean. With this new fuel supply, the captain hoped to steam through the barrier of drifting ice that was blocking his passage south, and then continue under sail.

When the crew learned the sad fate of my companions, they unanimously decided to head for Cape Grant and search for them as soon as they had taken on equipment and provisions.

Konrad was then brought on board, and Captain Sakharov invited us to take supper with him in the mess. The other guests were: Dr. P. Kushakov, Sedov's replacement as expedition leader; the geographer V. Vize; the geologist M. Pavlov; and the artist N. Pinegin. We were welcomed in a most princely manner. The menu consisted of delicious, crusty, white bread, fresh eggs, canned meat, and roast bearded seal, with a glass of vodka. Dessert was tea with milk and real sugar, and biscuits. We could not have been happier to be once again among our own people. But they seemed to have come from a world that was now quite foreign to us. There was a fine piano in the mess, and Mr. Vize played like a maestro. An excellent gramophone with a varied repertoire provided additional dinner music.

After dessert I asked our host to allow us to wash and, if possible, change our clothes, for all through the meal I had been in fear of seeing a louse crawl out of my sleeves. My request was immediately granted and minutes later we were the proud owners of a clean set of clothes.

Everyone had donated some item he could do without. In the engine room we transformed ourselves into new men from head to foot, after a good wash and a shave.

Surrounded by such kind and helpful friends, I suddenly felt I had a new lease on life, and an unfamiliar wave of happiness swept over me. It was as if we had already been repatriated, although we still had a very long way to go. The fact that the *Saint Foka* was crippled and could only make slow headway, due to the lack of fuel, did not worry us unduly. Then suddenly the engines came to life: I heard a rushing noise, the whistle of steam and the throbbing of the pump. The sole topic of conversation of those around us was "When will we reach the continent? When will we drop anchor in an inhabited harbor?"

I spent the evening with Dr. Kushakov, who gave me an up-to-date history of the expedition and its vicissitudes. Thus I learned that a detachment led by Vize had traveled to Cape Flora the previous winter, where they had dropped off the mail and spent a few days in the little hut which Konrad and I had occupied, thereby explaining the signs we had discovered of a recent visit. Vize had also been to Bell Island and I was greatly surprised to learn that on the northwest coast there was a hut built by Leigh Smith over forty years ago,* including a little storehouse of supplies and a good rowboat. If only I had known! To think that we had been only three hundred feet away from it when we were hunting for ducks' nests and exploring Eira Harbor. We had obviously turned back only moments before we would have stumbled across it.

* Actually thirty-four years earlier.

Those few steps we had not taken had very serious consequences. Had we discovered this hut, Lunayev and Shpakovsky would surely have been saved, and would be sitting alongside us now on board the *Saint Foka*. They would have rested in the hut and regained their strength. For Nilsen it would have been too late; he was already too close to death's door. Having found solace and fresh supplies in this refuge, we would have taken the sturdy rowboat across Mieres Channel, since we would have read the note Vize had left explaining the outcome of his expedition. We would also have avoided the storm and its distressing consequences. How wretched it is to learn such things when it is too late, when the irreparable damage has been done, and no amount of regret can change things! But I must admit that we had been dogged by the most extraordinary bad luck.

Sedov's men were astonished that I had not read their mail and asked me why. I could give them no real reason, but I think I was right in not doing so. I would have learned that the *Saint Foka* was anchored only forty miles away at Hooker Island, and that would have thrown me into great confusion, for I would not have been able to decide what to do.

Would we have gone to Hooker Island by kayak? The large whaleboat we found in storage on the beach would have been out of the question, as it was too big for two men to handle. We would also have assumed that the *Saint Foka* would be heading straight for home, without stopping at Cape Flora. We could not have left before the eighteenth of July: I was too sick before then. We would have followed a course up the Mieres Channel, where there was open water, especially since the eastern side of

Northbrook Island was totally unknown to us, and too open and unprotected. But it was precisely from that opposite, eastern coast that the *Saint Foka* had appeared on July 20. We would therefore have missed each other and reached Hooker Island after their departure, which would have been most depressing. Then we would have paddled the forty miles back, only to find our cabin at Cape Flora destroyed by the crew of the *Saint Foka*. So perhaps I saved our lives by not opening those mail cans!

The next morning, we all went ashore to dismantle the big cabin and transport the wood to the ship. All the provisions we had taken so much trouble to organize now had to be moved into our small hut. To these we added cans of food, biscuits, and other victuals, along with two rifles and five hundred cartridges off the *Saint Foka* for the benefit of any future lost sailors. Our comfortable "mansion" was soon transformed into an Arctic refuge.

It would be an exaggeration to say that everyone felt safe on board the *Saint Foka*. The shortage of fuel was very worrying, and frequent collisions with ice floes were a further source of concern. The ship was also very old, no longer very seaworthy, and had sprung a leak. Every day, each of us had to work the pumps for two three-hour shifts to prevent the ship from sinking.

JULY 23

Wind from the south-southwest. We have dropped anchor in Gunther Bay on the north coast of Northbrook Island. On the western shore we found a lifeboat in good condition, which we have taken on board in case we have to abandon ship.

JULY 25

The *Saint Foka* has finally got under way, after leaving notes sealed inside two tin cans on Northbrook Island: One contains a summary of my journey after my departure from the *Saint Anna;* in the other Dr. Kushakov relates the outcome of Sedov's expedition. The *Saint Foka* will now head for Cape Grant to search for my lost shipmates and then make for home without further delay.

Leaving Franz Josef Land

JULY 25

We weighed anchor at around nine in the evening and
started steaming for Cape Grant—not initially toward
Cape Grant, actually, but rather toward Bell Island, which
we would like to explore first, in case our companions had
stopped at the Eira Harbor hut.

We have enough fuel to last for three days, and we
must cover as much distance as possible during that
time—provided the ice does not stop us! We hope that the
wind remains favorable, so we do not need to rely entirely
on our engines.

SUNDAY, JULY 27

I had no time at all to devote to my diary yesterday: I was
on watch, and then slept for the rest of the day. Let us
bring things up to date.

We arrived at Bell Island at two in the morning on the
twenty-sixth, and Leigh Smith's hut, situated in an open,

low-lying area beside Eira Harbor, was clearly visible from quite a distance. I cannot fathom why we failed to see it the first time. It is made of planks, and in very good condition despite its age. We saw not a trace of our comrades. No one except us has since set foot on the island. We fired shots into the air and gave a few blasts of the ship's whistle to show that we were there but received no reply. So we then set sail for Cape Grant. Ice floes forced us to stand off the coast at a distance of four miles, and the best we could do was scan the shore through the binoculars and listen to the echoes of our shots and the ship's whistle ring through the air, but again our efforts were useless. Having done our duty to the best of our ability, we set a southerly course, first under sail, then later steam. By noon the islands of the archipelago had disappeared for good. We have now been sailing through open waters for twenty-four hours. Farewell, Cape Flora!

On the twenty-seventh, at around three in the morning, icebergs forced us to head west. They were not close together, but difficult to navigate through under sail. The temperature of the water was decreasing. Toward noon our calculations showed our latitude to be 78°23', an encouraging position. We have enough fuel left for thirty-six hours, and are making good headway under sail, although we have to tack among the icebergs. A mother polar bear and her cubs floated by on a floe. We sounded the whistle and the three of them immediately took to their heels.

There were four live polar bears on board the *Saint Foka,* three of which were already two years old, and they were so tame that the only reason they were kept in chains was that they got up to so much mischief if let loose—stealing, tearing things to bits, breaking everything in sight. They were not aggressive toward humans, unless provoked. They played with the dogs and during the inevitable quarrels that ensued, the dogs usually won. When the squabbles got out of hand, Mr. Pinegin would quickly restore the peace by cracking his whip a few times.

JULY 28

Until four in the morning, we sailed through a dense fog, tacking among the floes. At one point as we came about, the vessel collided with a large ice floe, and despite our best efforts we were not able to sail free of it. We put the ice anchor into use, and waited to see what would happen. By nine-thirty we were moving forward again under sail and steam and soon reached an open channel running to the south-southeast. By about noon we had reached latitude 77°48′. If we could run the engines for another day and a half, we would certainly get beyond the last of the sea ice; but we have sufficient fuel on hand for only another one and a half hours of steam. At this very moment the ship belowdecks is being ransacked: bulkheads, auxiliary beams, anything that is not a vital structural part of the ship is being mercilessly sacrificed to the ax. Not a single cabin was spared, and we will all have to spend the night on deck. Mr. Vize has even suggested feeding the piano to the flames. For the time being we cannot yet bring ourselves to do that, and hope to avoid such an act of vandalism. I have even heard that the jib boom and topmast will be next to be fed to the boiler.

JULY 29

Trapped in the ice! Yesterday evening at around eleven, the ice suddenly closed in so rapidly that it was impossible to get through, even under full power. We had to lash up to the ice with our ice anchor. Our deck made a strange dormitory, with crates and piles of firewood taking up most of the room.

JULY 31

Thick fog. Still imprisoned in the ice. We have dismantled the topmast, the jib boom, and the spritsail gaff and are busy sawing them up. Our boilers will soon devour the last piece of wood on board, and we are not yet out of this fix. Spare sails, coils of rope, mattresses, everything that is not absolutely necessary has been piled in the coal bins as a last resort. We are already seriously thinking of dismantling the rear deck. The leak in the hull is also adding to our daily worries. The water level in the hold has reached fifty inches or more. Since the bilge pump is not mechanical, we have to operate it manually without stopping.

The weather changed last night: The fog began to lift, the wind from the north lessened, and we drifted southward with the ice. During the night a cold northerly sprang up and by morning the fog had vanished.

At half past five in the morning, we weighed anchor, hoisted all the sails, and maintained a southerly heading. We encountered fewer and fewer ice floes, and our old ship managed to make an astonishing four to five knots. We have been economizing our steam power—so dearly paid for—as we will need it later, and for the moment we are able to cruise along under sail. Three hours later, the ice locked us in once more. We must be patient and wait. The wind has veered to the north; force 5.

AUGUST 6

My diary has had five days' rest. I have had no spare time to write it up, and more to the point, I would hardly have had any pleasure in describing these last few depressing days. The ice had closed in on all sides. There was such an accumulation of it that we thought we would never see our way free. We were already contemplating abandoning the vessel and heading for Novaya Zemlya with the big lifeboat. We had prepared food supplies two days previously. It would be impossible to spend the winter on board a vessel that was nothing but a hull and an engine, not to mention the lack of provisions. So we saw no other alternative. If the ship did not break free very shortly, we would have to try to reach Novaya Zemlya on foot, across the ice. After lengthy discussions, we resolved to wait a few more days, during which we would do everything possible to supplement our fuel supply. Then, if there were no change, the orders would be: Grease your boots, gentlemen, for a forced march to Novaya Zemlya, and look lively! Hardly an attractive prospect.

To make matters worse, the crew's present physical condition caused us to envision this possibility with fear and trepidation. Two of the men are almost paralyzed in the legs, as a result of the terrible past winters; they are crawling about on all fours, even though they are quite healthy otherwise. One of them is even working as a stoker. Finally, on the fourth, a brisk northwest breeze began to blow, it became noticeably colder, and the ice began to move. Yesterday a few polynyas began to form not far from the ship. To the south a water sky and an open lead were visible from the top of the mast, according to the captain, who climbed up to see for himself. So we stoked up the boilers and weighed anchor at around midnight. The ship began to make for the south, sails raised, engines running, and she managed to break her way through the last patches of ice. We maintained a good heading throughout the day, albeit slowly. Everything we could possibly burn was sacrificed: the small forward cabin, a number of cross beams from the middle deck, a barrel of tar which we had fortuitously forgotten, etc. But by nine o'clock the engines were out of action once more. A moderate wind drove us slightly farther south, but dropped suddenly, leaving the sails hanging limp from the yards.

However, we were not far from the open sea: The worst of the floes were now behind us. We could already feel we were approaching ice-free waters from the characteristic roll of the ship. For the sailor these rhythmic swells are a sure sign that the open sea is near. Scores of bearded seals gamboled in our wake, and flocks of fulmars wheeled overhead.

AUGUST 7

Dead calm all night long; toward morning, a gentle north-easterly sufficed to fill our sails and we were able to log almost one mile an hour. At noon, our position was 75°16′ north and 46°45′ east. The farther south we go, the smaller the size and number of the floes; they are now scattered over the broad, infinite face of the ocean and present no serious danger for the ship. The weather was fine, with a hazy glow floating on the horizon.

Finally, at around four in the afternoon, the long-awaited moment arrived when we left all the ice behind us. The high seas stretched before us in all their majestic immensity as far as the Murmansk coast, the most northerly point of the powerful Russian Empire. The waves shimmered with the deep blue typical of those regions where the Gulf Stream penetrates far into the Barents Sea. Praise God, we had now joined a heavily traveled maritime route and could maintain a straight course for Cape Svyatoy, the sacred cape at the entrance to the White Sea. We had abandoned our earlier plan to sail for Novaya Zemlya. It had not been an easy choice, for given the pitiful condition of the ship, it would have been more conservative to head for Novaya Zemlya, where we could have hugged the coast, collected loads of driftwood, and, if need be, ridden out any storms in one of that archipelago's sheltered bays.

But the desire to return home as rapidly as possible won the day; four hundred miles lay between Cape Svyatoy and us. We would be sailing across an open sea, in a virtually empty ship, without any ballast, which would add to our speed and, moreover, this latter route would shorten our journey by at least two hundred miles. These considerations decided it for us. The sailors were relieved of steering and only had to take turns at the pump, while the officers relayed each other at the helm.

All day long we had only a light breeze that scarcely filled our sails. But we were not unduly worried by this calm, for we knew that it was the season for northerly winds, which would pick up sooner or later.

AUGUST 8

Despite the lack of wind, the ship seems to be making headway, and we estimated that we must have crossed the 75th parallel this morning. Imagine our disappointment when at noon we found our position to be at 75°16', the very same latitude as twenty-four hours before. Our calculations were absolutely correct, so there must have been another reason, probably the influence of the Gulf Stream. At dawn, the water temperature was 28° Fahrenheit, at noon, 35° Fahrenheit, and in the evening, 38°. No sign of any ice! This morning, the wind was out of the northeast; during the day, it veered to the east. The ship is heeling sharply and our speed is increasing. Toward evening we were running at five knots. We hope to maintain this speed.

SUNDAY, AUGUST 10

It was all an illusion. Today we are at 74°18', and have not even covered one degree of latitude in twenty-four hours—again, no doubt, because of the strong currents. The temperature of the water is 42.5°. Whatever the reason may be, our progress is slow, and the winds are contrary.

On August 9 I was at the helm. A slight easterly wind barely filled the sails, and we were making roughly two miles an hour. It was very warm and I could hardly believe that only recently we had been besieged by thick ice and were contemplating trying to reach Novaya Zemlya on foot. We were drawing near the Murmansk coast, which we expected to appear out of the mist at any moment. I scrutinized the hazy horizon with the utmost attention, anxious to be the first to spot land or a vessel coming out to meet us. I had no time to become bored up on the bridge, for those who wanted to scan the horizon with the binoculars frequently came up to visit me. Each of us wanted to be the first to cry out, "Land Ho!"

Suddenly a dark, undulating shape stood out in the fog. I hesitated for a moment, looked closer, and easily recognized the distant shoreline as being the Murmansk coast. I let out a great cheer!

And yet we were all so tired of sailing at such a sluggish pace, after having dreamed of a steamship that would tow us as far as Arkhangel'sk, or at least lend us some coal. But no such vessel came out to greet us. We kept close watch on the horizon, ready for the moment when we could wave our flag. An hour after I had sighted land, we saw some small clouds of smoke rising in spirals on the horizon. Another hour went by before a long-awaited steamship came into view. But it was a Norwegian vessel on its way out of Arkhangel'sk with a heavy cargo of wood. They were heading in quite a different direction, and we doubted they would change course, since we were in fact under sail. Nonetheless, we hopefully hoisted our rather insignificant distress signal. The steamship passed by. We continued making for the coast, which slowly grew nearer, its shoreline becoming more and more distinct. However, we could not yet determine whether we were near the Kharkov light or at another point farther along the Murmansk coast. But when night fell we could see no

beam of light. We changed to a more southeasterly heading, skirting the coast. At about ten at night, when we had
just had supper, we saw the lights of another steamer. It
was advancing rapidly, lit up with electric lights, so that it
stood out clearly in the dark. It could only be one of the
passenger vessels of the Arkhangel'sk-Murmansk line,
plying between Arkhangel'sk and the local fishing ports,
and the Norwegian port of Vardø. We could not have
asked for more: If the captain were willing, they could tow
us to any port along the coast.

The *Saint Foka* hove to; we set off signal rockets and
also burned flares on the deck. We were sure that the
steamship could not possibly fail to see our signals, and
would come to investigate. But not at all! Dumbfounded,
we looked at each other in silence. It went on its way,
paying not the slightest attention. We made a final attempt by lighting packets of oakum soaked in kerosene
up on the fo'c'sle, which seemed to plunge our old tub
into a sea of flames. But the ferry continued to ignore us
and steamed steadily on. What else could we do? As a last
resort, we shot off a few rounds from our whaling guns. A
veritable bombardment, with our gunners firing away as
if they were on a practice range!

This last attempt certainly had an effect, but not the
one we anticipated. The steamship, still not too far away,
suddenly vanished. We stared in wide-eyed amazement:
Had it really been a ship? Yes, but it had put out all its
lights in the twinkling of an eye and disappeared into the
night. This took us completely by surprise and for a moment we were speechless; then simultaneously all the men
roundly abused the lily-livered captain who had not

deemed our distress worthy of his attention. And a Russian steamship to boot! The conduct of the foreign vessel had not worried us unduly, for it was a long way off the coast, and we were not altogether certain that it had seen us. But the Russian vessel was another situation altogether: The cowardly fellow had purposely shirked his duty, and his conduct was not just strange, but ignominious.

Our captain looked for all possible explanations and came up with the following: When Russian fishermen—*pomori*—are drunk, they light distress signals in their boats, something which often deceives other ships. When the rescue vessel comes alongside, the fishermen's so-called plight turns out to be a false alarm, and no one in particular can be held responsible, as the crew are all completely drunk. Naturally, captains who have fallen for this prank learn to pay no attention to such signals near the coast. But this explanation did not satisfy us. A ship that sets off an entire series of distress signals, even along the coast, should simply not be ignored and left to the mercy of a capricious captain's imagination. This is in complete contradiction to the long-established laws of the sea. Fortunately, we were not exactly in great danger. Since we could not obtain any fuel, we would just have to continue at our snail's pace, whether we liked it or not, and that is what we did, all night long.

At dawn we saw that we must have gone past the Kharkov lighthouse during the night. Because we were heading into wind, it did not seem wise to continue under sail as far as Arkhangel'sk, so we decided to make landfall at the first port where we could send a wire to request the help we had so far solicited in vain.

Near the fishing village of Rynda we met a fishing boat, a "snail," as they are called, with several men aboard: These were the first people any of us had seen since our departure two years previously. They had recognized the old *Saint Foka* from a long way off; they were to be our messengers of fate, and greeted us with very sad news from home. As if anticipating some misfortune, we asked: Tell us what is happening in the world! Has a war broken out in our absence? They looked at us with consternation, then cried out in unison: What? Haven't you heard that a terrible war has broken out, a war that started in Serbia? Germans, Austrians, French, English, Serbs, almost everyone is now involved in this violent conflict.

And what about Russia? we went on, overwhelmed by what we had just learned.

Of course Russia is fighting as well, allied to France, they answered. So it is a European war, one of us cried out. That's right, that's what they call it, said one of the fishermen. They passed on other interesting items of news, and also told us that the steamship that had so shamefully let us down the day before had been the *Lomonossov*. And then we understood. They had taken our poor old boat for an enemy warship and had fled as quickly as possible! Apparently the Murmansk coast was liable to be attacked at any time of the day or night by German submarines. We were certainly in the danger zone.

The fishermen kindly gave us some fresh milk and two pouches of tobacco that were very welcome to us all, although especially so to Sedov's men, who had done without for so long. In exchange, Dr. Kushakov gave the fishermen a bottle of rum, totally ignorant of the enormous price it would fetch in those war-torn times.

Dr. Kushakov went on board one of the fishing boats returning to Rynda, to send a wire announcing our arrival and requesting assistance. We could not maneuver into Rynda, as there was not enough wind. At four in the afternoon, two motorboats belonging to the Skobelev fishing company came alongside. Mr. Skobelev himself came to greet us and brought us a big pile of newspapers with the latest news of the war. Once the crews had become introduced, the two boats towed the *Saint Foka* into the port.

Among the news items in the newspapers, we read that the Russian government had organized two expeditions to look for Brusilov and Sedov. One had been sent to the Kara Sea and the other to Franz Josef Land, to search for the *Saint Foka*. That evening we all gathered in the telegraph office at Rynda, while Dr. Kushakov sent a number of telegrams. He was richer than any of us, having several hundred rubles in his possession. Then Konrad arrived with a pound sterling he had previously found on board the *Saint Anna* when he was dismantling the cabins! The rest of us, including me, did not have a kopeck to our names. Dr. Kushakov gave us credit, though, and paid for all of our telegrams. Everyone asked his family to send money.

On that same eventful day, Mr. Skobelev invited us to tea, and we learned that the S.S. *Emperor Nicholas II*, en route from Alexandrovsk to Arkhangel'sk, could take us on board. The next day, five men from the *Saint Foka* went on to Arkhangel'sk: apart from myself, there were Pavlov, Vize, Pinegin, and Konrad. The captain of the steamer could not have been more considerate. Not only did he allow us to travel free of charge, but he also provided our meals on credit during the entire passage and even gave us his own cabin, as the ship was fully booked.

This, then, was my homecoming after an odyssey that had lasted for two years. Of all the companions who left St. Petersburg on July 28, 1912, on board the *Saint Anna*, only two of us had returned. Miraculously rescued after so many hardships, we finally disembarked in Arkhangel'sk on September 1, 1914.

ACKNOWLEDGMENTS

Our primary debt of gratitude is to Christian de Marliave, the French polar expert who first called modern Western attention to Albanov's remarkable work. De Marliave bent the ear of his longtime friend, Michel Guérin, who in 1998 published a deluxe illustrated edition of the French version of the book, titled *Au pays de la mort blanche.*

It was through Guérin that one of us (Roberts) grew sufficiently intrigued to locate a rare library copy of the French edition and read it. The present edition, the first to appear in English, was translated from the French and then emended by corroboration with an unpublished literal translation from the original Russian that we were lucky enough to come across. We are grateful to our translators, Alison Anderson and Linda Dubosson, for their diligent and thorough renderings under intense deadline pressures. Christian de Marliave also served as an invaluable consultant during the process. To retired Canadian geography professor William Barr, who is probably the leading English-language expert on the history of Russian Arctic exploration, we owe an immense debt for making his verbatim translation from the Russian available, for creating the maps from which we have adapted ours, and for correcting such errors of detail as would otherwise have crept into our text.

Lee Boudreaux at Random House had the canny publisher's instinct to authorize this first English edition even before she had read the text, and she has scrupulously superintended our work on the book ever since. At Random House, Ann Godoff, David Ebershoff, and Brian McLendon instantly recognized Albanov's text as a classic, paving the way for launching the book in the U.S. with the éclat it deserves. Dennis Ambrose at Random House supervised the editorial production of the book with an elegant regard for accuracy and style. Editors Stephen Byers, John Rasmus, and Mark Jannot at *National Geographic Adventure* likewise seized on Albanov's achievement, producing a handsome first-serial excerpt to coincide with the book's publication.

John Ware, who acted as our agent on this project, was enthusiastic about Albanov from the beginning. Finally, to all the editors—they know who they are—who indulged our obsession with Albanov while it delayed and threatened to derail other work we had already committed to, we owe a vote of thanks for their forbearance.

—*Jon Krakauer and David Roberts*

Index

ABOUT THE AUTHOR

VALERIAN IVANOVICH ALBANOV was born in 1881 in the city of Voronezh, near the Don River in central Russia, some three hundred miles south of Moscow. His father, a veterinarian, died when Albanov was a young child, so he was raised by an uncle who lived in Ufa, a port on the Belaya River in the southwestern Urals. Mesmerized by seafaring tales from an early age, Albanov embarked on his first maritime adventure while still a schoolboy, but was forced to return home when his small craft sank. Though his uncle wanted him to become an engineer, Albanov was determined to study navigation, and at the age of seventeen he entered the Naval College at St. Petersburg. During the four years he spent as a student there, he supported himself by building scale models of ships. Upon graduation in 1904, Albanov trained on various vessels in the Baltic Sea before traveling to Krasnoyarsk in central Siberia, where he sailed down the Yenisei River to the Kara Sea as a first officer on the steamer *Ob*. From 1909 through 1911 he made numerous voyages between Arkhangel'sk and British ports aboard the steamship *Kildin.*

Then, in 1912, Albanov signed on as navigator of the schooner *Saint Anna,* under the command of Captain Georgiy Brusilov, bound for Vladivostok across the Northeast Passage—the ill-starred voyage that is recounted so vividly in these pages. Even before Albanov and Alexander Konrad fought their way back to civilization and told of the plight of their icebound shipmates, a number of search parties (including one headed by the seasoned Arctic explorer Otto Sverdrup) set out to find the *Saint Anna* but failed to turn up any trace of the ship. In October 1914 Albanov met the hydrographer Leonid Breitfuss, who persuaded him to write an account of the astounding ordeal he had just endured. Albanov's memoir, originally titled *Na iug, k Zemle Frantsa Iosifa* (*Southbound to Franz Josef Land*), was published in St. Petersburg in 1917, on the eve of the October Revolution, as an appendix to the journal *Zapisok po gidrografii* (*Notes on Hydrography*). Various editions of the work subsequently appeared in Russian as *Mezhdu zhizniu i smertiu* (*Between Life and Death,* 1925), *Zateriannye vo ldakh* (*Lost in the Ice,* 1934 and 1978), and *Podvigi shturmana V. I. Albanova* (*The Exploits of the Navigator V. I. Albanov,* 1953). It was also translated into German as *Irrfahrten im Lande des weissen Todes* (*Travels in the Land of White Death,* 1925) and later into French as *Au pays de la mort blanche* (*In the Land of White Death,* 1928 and 1998). More recently, Albanov's postexpedition letters were published in the journal *Letopis severa* (*Northern Memoirs;* Moscow, 1985, 11:174–81).

Despite his harrowing escape from the *Saint Anna,* Albanov continued going to sea. For a time he served with his fellow survivor Konrad aboard the *Canada,* an ice-breaker that serviced the port of Arkhangel'sk. Following a brief stay in a military hospital in St. Petersburg, he also sailed on ships from the Baltic ports of Tallinn and Haap-salu, and from Krasnoyarsk on the Yenisei River. Valerian Albanov died in the fall of 1919. By some accounts he succumbed to typhoid; other sources report that he was killed when a munitions wagon exploded as he was passing through a railway station in the Siberian town of Achinsk.

On the thirtieth anniversary of Albanov's death, the noted Russian geographer and Arctic explorer Vladimir Vize (who was aboard the *Saint Foka* when that ship rescued Albanov) paid him this tribute in the journal *Letopis severa* (*Northern Memoirs;* Moscow, 1949, 1:279–81): "Albanov owed his survival to his personal qualities: bravery, energy, and strong will.... His book, with its intriguing drama and fascinating simplicity and sincerity, is among the most prominent writings about the Arctic in Russian literature."

In 1975, Arctic expert William Barr wrote, "The name of Valerian Ivanovich Albanov must be ranked among those of the immortals of polar exploration."